"A fabulous tool. One of the best books I've read on teen social anxiety!"

> —**Lisa M. Schab, LCSW**, psychotherapist, and author of
> self-help books, including *The Anxiety Workbook for Te[*
> guided anxiety journal for teens, *Put Your Worries He[*

"With the second edition of her book, Jennifer Shannon has taken all the amazing tips and insights from the first edition and put them into the media-saturated context of teens today. The engaging illustrations and easy-to-understand tools make this an approachable resource for even the most anxious of teens."

> —**Litsa R. Tanner, MS, MFT,** clinical director and cofounder of
> the Santa Rosa Center for Cognitive Behavioral Therapy, and adjunct
> professor in counseling psychology at the University of San Francisco

"This workbook is fantastic! If you read it carefully, collaborate with the material, and do the exercises, you will get better. It's easy to follow, with wonderful illustrations and relatable stories. Social anxiety is not a life sentence. Jennifer Shannon's book will walk you through the steps you need to take to overcome your fears and feel comfortable in social situations."

> —**Ken Goodman, LCSW**, creator of *The Anxiety Solution Series*, and
> author of *The Emetophobia Manual*

"Jennifer Shannon, an expert in the treatment of anxiety, provides a practical and engaging update of *The Shyness and Social Anxiety Workbook for Teens*. She offers a straightforward and evidence-based approach with strategies that are all eminently doable. The chapter on social perfectionism—on overcoming the belief that one can't ever make mistakes—is particularly compelling. And, as a bonus, illustrations highlighting the key points further enhance the content."

> —**Mary K. Alvord, PhD**, psychologist, and coauthor of *Conquer Negative
> Thinking for Teens* and *Resilience Builder Program for Children and Adolescents*

"I loved the first edition, and this update is even better! Jennifer Shannon offers a clear guide to undoing the inhibiting effects social anxiety, and social media, can have on teens making their way in school and the world. The illustrations speak thousands of words! She charts a direct path to leaving shyness and loneliness behind. Let her be your guide."

> —**David Carbonell, PhD**, creator of www.anxietycoach.com, and author of *Panic Attacks Workbook*, *The Worry Trick*, *Fear of Flying Workbook*, and *Outsmart Your Anxious Brain*

"The new edition of *The Shyness and Social Anxiety Workbook for Teens* is a gift for teens and therapists alike. Jennifer Shannon presents evidence-based cognitive behavioral principles and practices with empathy and warmth, and the dynamic, comic book-like illustrations really bring the concepts to life. Teens who complete this workbook are sure to understand their social anxiety better—and how to move through it to a more fulfilling life."

> —**Seth J. Gillihan, PhD**, clinical psychologist, and coauthor of *CBT Deck for Kids and Teens*

the shyness & social anxiety workbook for teens

SECOND EDITION

CBT & ACT skills to help you build social confidence

JENNIFER SHANNON, LMFT

ILLUSTRATIONS BY DOUG SHANNON

Instant Help Books
An Imprint of New Harbinger Publications, Inc.

Publisher's Note

Distributed in Canada by Raincoast Books

Copyright © 2022 by Jennifer Shannon
     Instant Help Books
     An imprint of New Harbinger Publications, Inc.
     5674 Shattuck Avenue
     Oakland, CA 94609
     www.newharbinger.com

Illustrations by Doug Shannon

Cover design by Amy Shoup

Acquired by Tesilya Hanauer

Library of Congress Cataloging-in-Publication Data

Names: Shannon, Jennifer, author. | Shannon, Doug, illustrator.
Title: The shyness & social anxiety workbook for teens : CBT and ACT skills to help you build social
  confidence / Jennifer Shannon ; illustrations by Doug Shannon.
Description: Second edition. | Oakland, CA : Instant Help Books, an imprint of New Harbinger
  Publications, Inc., [2022] | Audience: Ages 13-19 | Audience: Grades 7-9
Identifiers: LCCN 2021043155 | ISBN 9781684038015 (trade paperback)
Subjects: LCSH: Bashfulness in adolescence--Juvenile literature. | Social phobia in adolescence--
  Juvenile literature. | Cognitive therapy for teenagers--Problems, exercises, etc. | Acceptance and
  commitment therapy--Problems, exercises, etc.
Classification: LCC BF575.B3 S5193 2022 | DDC 155.2/32--dc23/eng/20211115
LC record available at https://lccn.loc.gov/2021043155

Printed in the United States of America

25 24 23

10 9 8 7 6 5 4 3 2

Contents

Introduction

When the first edition of this book was published in 2012, social media was still, relatively speaking, in its infancy. It has since grown into a socializing tool that has transformed our lives and culture. As early adopters of many of the newest platforms, the teens of today face some new challenges.

Because social media posts and comments are public and can live online permanently, today's teens risk being criticized in ways that previous generations have not. The carefully chosen images and posts in social media streams can give the impression that others are always doing fun things in groups, triggering feelings of being left out or rejected. The negative judgments and social comparisons that social media can foster are directly linked to increased levels of social anxiety and depression among teens.

This new edition teaches teens how to master the negative thoughts and feelings that social media engagement can evoke. They'll learn how to adjust their expectations, both of others and themselves. They will learn how to cope with online criticism and the internalized criticism that results from it. All the insight and instruction from the first edition is still here, enhanced with new illustrations.

There is no reason to suffer with social anxiety. Help is here. If you're willing to work, this is the book for you.

Chapter 1

Socially Anxious
Are You Missing Out?

When you are at school, at a party, or on social media, do you worry that people might think that something you say or do is stupid or dumb? Do you compare yourself to others who you think are smarter, more attractive, more popular? Are you easily shamed or embarrassed? Do you worry that others can tell that you're anxious from your physical signs, like blushing, shaking, or sweating?

Being concerned about being observed and judged by others is normal for teenagers. Feeling awkward and anxious a lot of the time is normal too. But for some teens, anxiety in social situations is a problem that is disrupting their lives. Here are five socially anxious teens who will help you understand your own shyness and what you can do about it. Alex doesn't date because he's worried he won't know what to say. Bella avoids being the center of attention because she blushes, which will let everybody know she's anxious. Brandi is worried about being judged on social media, and she spends hours trying to perfect her posts. Lucia isn't confident she has much to contribute in conversation, so she doesn't say anything. And Chris is worried about making a mistake in a variety of situations where he may be observed. In this workbook, we'll follow along with these, and other teens, as they learn to master their social anxiety.

Here are some common social situations that can trigger anxiety. Check each one that makes you feel anxious.

☐ Starting or joining a conversation

☐ Answering questions in class

☐ Inviting a friend to get together

☐ Taking a test

☐ Initiating a text to someone you don't know well

☐ Entering a room where others are already seated

☐ Writing on the whiteboard or chalkboard

☐ Posting comments or photos on social media

☐ Working with a group of teens

☐ Participating in P.E. class

☐ Creating a social media profile

☐ Walking in the hallways or hanging out by your locker

☐ Asking a teacher a question, or for help

☐ Responding to a text someone sent you

☐ Using school or public bathrooms

☐ Eating in front of others

☐ Writing in front of others

☐ Answering or talking on the phone

☐ Performing in public

☐ Giving a report or reading aloud in front of the class

☐ Speaking to adults (for example, store clerks, waiters, or your principal)

☐ Talking to new or unfamiliar people

☐ Attending parties, dances, or school activity nights

☐ Having your picture taken (for example, for your school yearbook)

☐ Dating

You've probably identified with several, even many, of these anxiety-triggering situations. Does that mean you have a problem? Not necessarily. The real test of your social anxiety is not whether you get anxious in social situations, but whether you go out of your way to *avoid* those situations.

THE REAL TEST IS NOT WHETHER YOU FEEL ANXIOUS...

...IT'S WHETHER YOU GO OUT OF YOUR WAY TO AVOID FEELING ANXIOUS.

You can live with social anxiety by avoiding situations that make you uncomfortable, but if you're like most socially anxious teens, you're tired of missing out. This workbook is designed to help you get back what you're missing and reclaim your life.

To help you identify whether you suffer from social anxiety, you can take a quiz at http://www.newharbinger.com/48015. (See the very back of this book for more information about downloads.) Turn to the next chapter to learn how social anxiety develops and why it isn't your fault.

Chapter 2

Why Me?

The Origins of Social Anxiety

To understand your own social anxiety, you'll need to understand where it comes from and the purpose it serves. Our social connections feel super important to us for a very good reason. They *are* super important. With few exceptions, a lone human being cannot survive for long. From our earliest recorded history, we've been social animals, building shelter from the weather, hunting and gathering food, and fighting off predators *together*, in families, tribes, and communities.

Because our relationships with others are so important to our survival, our body's central nervous system works hard to prevent us from making mistakes that could lead to criticism and rejection. In a social situation where we might bore or offend someone, we experience anxiety—delivered by our nervous system—in the form of fear, embarrassment, tension, sweating, and other sensations. The purpose of anxiety is to alert us not to take unnecessary social risks that could threaten our relationships with people we rely on to survive and thrive.

As helpful and necessary as anxiety is, for some of us, our body's nervous system is overreactive, dialed up so high that we get false alarms. Like a smoke sensor that goes off whenever you're using the toaster, your anxiety may be signaling false alarms, exaggerating the danger of you being criticized and rejected.

It would be convenient if we could dial down our nervous system to be less reactive, but the part of our brain that runs our nervous system is hardwired to be out of our direct control, with a mind of its own. Being the oldest, simplest, most primitive part of our brain, it can't reason or assess risk like the logical, rational part of our brain can. It "thinks" more like an animal, instinctively and reactively.

While it is often referred to as the "reptile brain" or the "lizard brain," I prefer to call this animalistic part of our brain the "monkey mind." Unlike reptiles and lizards, monkeys are social animals who care about belonging and will do anything to avoid getting kicked out of their tribe.

If you're avoiding social situations you wish you could engage in, but cannot because it feels like your very survival depends on avoiding them, you have an overreactive *monkey mind*. It overestimates the likelihood of others judging you negatively and it underestimates your ability to cope with negative judgments when they do occur. Which brings us to the question: Why is there a wild little beast running *your* nervous system, and not everybody else's?

You didn't invent this problem for yourself. There are three things that can influence how reactive your nervous system is in social situations. The first is your *genetic disposition*.

Genetic Disposition

We come into this world with predetermined traits, including the tendency toward anxiety in social situations. If you examine your family history, you will likely find an uncle or aunt, a parent or grandparent, even a sibling with shyness like you. They may not have had full-fledged social anxiety, but they were "dialed up" in a way you might recognize. Scientists haven't discovered a specific shyness gene yet, but they have determined that, like blue eyes or curly hair, social anxiety is passed down generation to generation[*].

List any of your relatives who show anxiety in social situations.

_____

_____

_____

_____

* *In addition to shyness, there are a variety of other of anxiety problems you or your relatives may have experienced. In the appendix at the end of the book, there is a list of these common anxieties.*

Parental Modeling

The second factor that might contribute to your social anxiety is *parental modeling*. Do your parents rarely socialize? Are they highly invested in making a good impression? If your parents are overly cautious or reclusive, you may have learned some of your socially anxious behavior from them.

Describe any ways that your parents model anxiety and avoidance.

_____

_____

_____

_____

_____

_____

_____

_____

Upsetting Events

Almost everyone has experienced forgetting their lines in a school presentation or play. For most people, the experience is a memory to chuckle over, but for the socially anxious it may have been a traumatic disaster. They are so worried about a repeat performance that being called upon in class or doing an oral presentation is genuinely terrifying.

Your own personal *upsetting event* could have been giving the wrong answer in class, finding out you weren't invited to a party when everyone else was, hearing a rumor that you liked a classmate you really didn't, or having a mean teacher who shamed you in front of the class.

What upsetting events stand out in your memory?

_____

_____

_____

_____

_____

_____

_____

_____

You can't change your genealogy, your parents, or your past. What you *can* change is how you respond to anxiety *now*. What you do in social situations today will determine how you feel in social situations in the future. That's because your brain, even the primitive, stubborn part of it, is still learning all the time. Like its namesake, the monkey mind can be tamed.

Throughout this book, you will see illustrations of different teens with a monkey. These are to remind you that regardless of how your social anxiety developed, the way to master it is by mastering the monkey mind. To learn how, turn to the next chapter.

Chapter 3

Chain Reaction

*Automatic Thoughts, Anxious Feelings,
and Avoidance*

Alex

Alex notices Ginelle, whom he finds attractive, approaching in the hall. He quickly buries his head in his locker as if he were looking for a book. Within a few seconds, Ginelle turns the corner and is gone.

Alex stuck his head in his locker, apparently to avoid contact with someone he is actually attracted to. Is this in Alex's best interest? Why would Alex act in a way that reduces his chances of getting to know someone he likes?

To understand why Alex avoided Ginelle, we'll have to break down the scene and identify the links in the chain of events. Let's replay the sequence and freeze-frame on the moment Alex first saw Ginelle to see what he was thinking.

Automatic Thoughts

The thoughts that flashed through Alex's mind when he saw her approach—that if he didn't say something clever to impress her, she'd think he was weird, stupid, less than good enough—were familiar to him. He'd had similar thoughts many times before, not just about Ginelle, but about anybody he was impressed with or attracted to.

The theme of socially anxious teens' thoughts is always that other people are watching and judging them. They think they need to perform to a high standard or they'll be criticized or laughed at, either openly or behind their back. These thoughts happen automatically, so quickly that we're often not even aware of them.

Triggered Feelings

These automatic thoughts then trigger how we feel. If you were like Alex, thinking that unless you were clever, you'd be seen as stupid or weird, how would *you* feel?

Here are some common emotions that socially anxious teens feel:

Embarrassed—humiliated, self-conscious

Anxious—worried, panicky, nervous, frightened

Lonely—alone

Hopeless—discouraged, defeated

Ashamed—remorseful

Guilty—bad, sorry

Sad—depressed, down, unhappy

Frustrated—stuck, thwarted, defeated

Jealous—envious, distrustful

Confused—befuddled, confounded, lost

Hurt—wounded, upset, injured

Disappointed—let down, disillusioned, disheartened

Angry—mad, resentful, irritated, upset

If we asked Alex what he was feeling, he might describe his discomfort with a word like "anxious," "panicky," "insecure," "embarrassed," or just plain "scared." What's the natural thing to do when we feel this way?

What we've done ever since the first caveman confronted a mountain lion: run away and hide!

Avoidance Behavior

When people face situations that make them feel anxious, *avoidance* is the most common action they take. Avoidance prevents the thing that they are afraid will happen from happening. Alex is anxious that he won't know what to say to Ginelle and she'll think he's weird. If he hides in his locker, there is no risk of this happening. It's a foolproof short-term solution to his social anxiety.

The problem? In the long run, Alex never gets what he really wants, which is to get to know Ginelle. He ends up missing out on that relationship, which leads to loneliness and depression.

Bella

Bella is attending the first meeting of her class's yearbook committee. Everybody is taking turns introducing themselves and what they are interested in contributing.

While others were introducing themselves, Bella was so anxious, she could barely focus on what they were saying. The closer it came for her turn, the faster her heart beat and the redder her face grew.

When her moment arrived, she covered her face and said as little as possible. Bella really wanted to be part of the yearbook committee, but her anxiety got in the way of participating in the group. To understand what triggered her anxiety, let's zero in on what she was thinking as her turn approached.

Automatic Thoughts

Bella's prediction that everyone would notice her blushing and shaky voice wasn't planned; it happened automatically. Anytime she had to express herself in a new situation, she had those thoughts. The possibility of others' observing and judging her triggered strong feelings in Bella, just as they did with Alex. What would you feel if you thought others would notice how anxious you were? Embarrassed? Ashamed?

Physical Sensations

Emotions like shame and embarrassment that are triggered by our automatic thoughts are often accompanied by another kind of anxious feeling: strong physical sensations. Here are some common ones that you may have experienced.

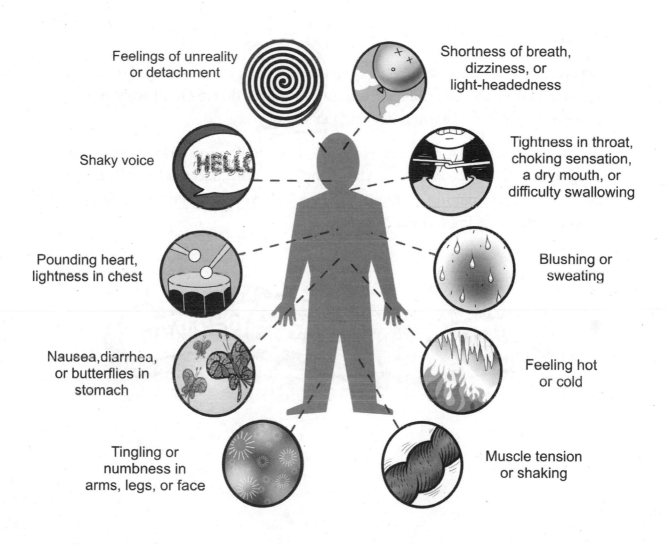

Feelings of unreality or detachment

Shortness of breath, dizziness, or light-headedness

Shaky voice

HELLO

Tightness in throat, choking sensation, a dry mouth, or difficulty swallowing

Pounding heart, lightness in chest

Blushing or sweating

Nausea, diarrhea, or butterflies in stomach

Feeling hot or cold

Tingling or numbness in arms, legs, or face

Muscle tension or shaking

While physical sensations like these are perfectly normal, for teens like Bella, thinking that others will notice and judge them is especially troubling. Have you ever worried that people would notice that you were sweating, blushing, or that your hands and voice were shaking, and negatively judge you? We're much more aware of our own physical symptoms than others are, but it certainly doesn't feel that way.

Avoidance Behavior

When we feel strongly that being seen is dangerous to our social standing, we avoid being seen. For Bella, the natural thing to do was to prevent others from seeing her red face and hearing her shaky voice.

Just as we saw with Alex, when we break down Bella's scenario, we observe a chain reaction. *Automatic thoughts* ("They'll see how anxious I am!") trigger *anxious feelings* (blushing, tight throat), which provoke *avoidance behavior* (covering face, saying as little as possible).

While avoidance behavior is a reliable short-term solution to our anxious feelings, it fails to deliver what we truly want and need: connection and belonging. Where it ultimately takes us is to isolation and depression. In order to break this chain reaction, you'll need to examine how it works in your own life, the topic of the next chapter.

Chapter 4

Slowing It Down

Recognizing Your Own Chain Reactions

As we learned in the last chapter, the emotions and sensations that make us want to avoid social situations wouldn't happen without the automatic thoughts that trigger them. If only we could prevent automatic thoughts from popping up, there would be no chain reaction!

But as long as we keep avoiding the situations that make us socially anxious, negative automatic thoughts about those situations will keep occurring. That's because avoidance behavior is what makes automatic thoughts so believable. Every time Alex avoids Ginelle, or anyone he's attracted to, he is confirming to himself that to approach her would be dangerous. Every time Bella covers up in a social situation, she confirms to herself how bad it will be if others see she's anxious.

It works just the same for you as it does for Alex and Bella. Avoiding any social situation confirms that the situation *is* indeed dangerous. And when we continuously avoid situations, we never learn how to cope when someone does criticize or judge us. Regular confirmations that a situation is too dangerous for you encourage more scary automatic thoughts about that situation the next time it happens. This chain reaction repeats itself again and again, making avoidance a regular habit, and leading to a lifetime of missing out.

While it may sound hopeless when put this way, as you will learn, it's great news. Once you can identify the chain reactions in your own life, you can begin planning how to break them. Let's look at some more common social anxiety triggering scenarios for teens. See if you can identify the chain reaction at work in each of them.

Lucia

Let's review Lucia's thought-feeling-behavior chain in this situation, writing down what you think she was thinking, feeling, and doing.

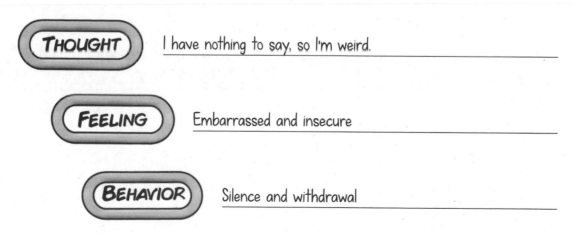

THOUGHT — I have nothing to say, so I'm weird.

FEELING — Embarrassed and insecure

BEHAVIOR — Silence and withdrawal

Have you ever been with a group of people who are conversing about something you don't know much about? Write down an example here.

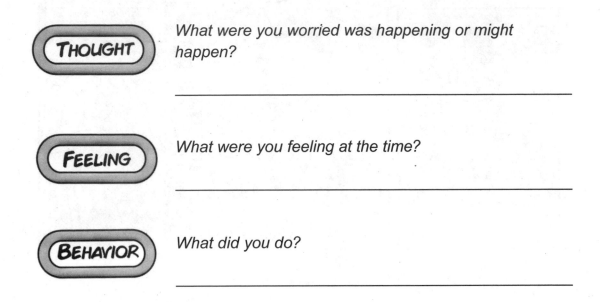

THOUGHT — *What were you worried was happening or might happen?*

_____

FEELING — *What were you feeling at the time?*

_____

BEHAVIOR — *What did you do?*

_____

Let's look at some experiences of other teens and see if we can spot the chain reaction.

Brandi

What is Brandi's thought-feeling-behavior chain?

THOUGHT _____

FEELING _____

BEHAVIOR _____

Do you think others are judging your posts and other social media activity?

_____

What do you think they might be thinking or saying?

_____

_____

_____

_____

How do you avoid being judged negatively on social media?

_____

_____

_____

_____

Chris

Here's a situation that triggers Chris's anxiety. He thinks he's alone with this problem, but many teens become self-conscious doing ordinary activities when others are around.

Write down Chris's thought-feeling-behavior chain.

THOUGHT _____

FEELING _____

BEHAVIOR _____

Some things that we can do perfectly naturally when we're alone seem impossible in the presence of others. What's a situation that makes you self-conscious?

_____

_____

How do you think others would judge your "performance"?

_____

_____

How do those real or imagined judgments make you feel?

_____

_____

What do those feelings make you want to do?

_____

_____

This next exercise will help you examine your own thought-feeling-behavior chains in more detail. A copy of this worksheet is also available at http://www.newharbinger.com/48015.

Go back to the list on page 3 and look at the situations you checked that make you anxious. Pick out a couple that are especially a problem for you, then see how well you can describe each link of your chain reaction in the space below.

Situation 1: _____

(THOUGHT)   _____

(FEELING)   _____

(BEHAVIOR)   _____

Situation 2: _____

(THOUGHT)   _____

(FEELING)   _____

(BEHAVIOR)   _____

31

Our thought-feeling-behavior chain reactions happen so quickly in anxious situations that we often find ourselves at the avoidance behavior link before we know what happened. Just as a baseball batter develops the ability to see the ball traveling at ninety miles an hour, we can develop awareness of our automatic thoughts and anxious feelings, and slow down the chain to where we can get a handle on it.

A chain is only as strong as its weakest link. If you can identify the links, you can learn how to go about breaking the chain. In the next chapter, we'll take a good hard look at our automatic thoughts.

Chapter 5

Disastrous Distortions

Don't Believe Every Thought You Think

Imagine you are looking at yourself in a funhouse mirror at a carnival or fair. Yes, that is you, but your face is not that long, your stomach is not that fat, and your legs are not that skinny. The mirror is distorting the reality of what is there.

When we are anxious, our thoughts reflect in a funhouse mirror. Worse still, we are unaware of the distortion and take those thoughts at face value, making us even more scared.

This chapter explains six examples of distorted thinking that people with social anxiety commonly experience. When you recognize the distortion in your thoughts, it becomes easier to take them less seriously. The first distortion is one you'll recognize right away.

Catastrophizing

You've probably heard people ask, what's the worst that can happen? When a trigger situation occurs, and you jump to the worst possible outcome—even though there are a hundred other possible outcomes—you are *catastrophizing*.

When this teen is turned down for a date, he assumes it is so newsworthy that the whole school will soon know and be laughing at him. While that might qualify as a catastrophe, how likely is it to happen?

Tell about a situation in your own life where you catastrophized.

_____

_____

_____

_____

_____

_____

What was the worst possible outcome that you assumed would happen?

_____

_____

_____

_____

_____

Discounting the Positive

Do you ever worry so much about one thing you said or did that you forget the fact that, overall, your social interaction went well? Say that you were talking to someone and, instead of getting all tongue-tied, you actually enjoyed the conversation. Instead of feeling good that sometimes you really *do* have something to talk about, you conclude: "Well, she's really nice, and that's why I felt comfortable, but most people aren't like that and I'd totally freeze up talking with them." It is difficult to develop confidence when you ignore your successes, when you *discount the positive*.

Jonathan told a funny joke that his friends laughed at, but instead of enjoying their response and giving himself credit for being funny, he focuses on the possibility that he may have been misunderstood.

Describe a social situation that basically went well, and you replayed it in your head over and over, looking for where you made a mistake.

_____

_____

_____

_____

_____

What was positive about your interaction with others that you discounted?

_____

_____

_____

People who see the good in everything are sometimes said to be wearing rose-colored glasses. A socially anxious teen in a trigger situation could be said to be wearing gray-colored glasses. All their senses are working and they are taking everything in, but they discount all the information that is positive, leaving only the negative. Here's another teen who can't see what is working for them.

In what situations do you seem able to see only what isn't working?

_____

_____

_____

_____

_____

Labeling

Sticks and stones may break your bones, but words can *really* harm you. By calling someone else names, you are degrading that person. Calling yourself names degrades you. For example, you drop your books in the hall, and you tell yourself you are lame. But we've all made clumsy mistakes. Are we all lame?

Losing a game of chess doesn't make you a loser. Blurting out a silly idea doesn't make you an idiot. Words like "lame" and "loser" and "idiot" are *labels* that don't really explain the whole of who we are.

Socially anxious teens often use labels like these to describe themselves. Which do you use on yourself?

☐ Pathetic   ☐ Boring

☐ Stupid   ☐ Jerk

☐ Hopeless   ☐ Loser

☐ Defective   ☐ Lame

☐ Incompetent   ☐ Disgusting

☐ Idiot   ☐ Crazy

Spotlighting

When a great golfer is driving the ball off the tee in a close match, they aren't thinking about their grip on the club or the arc of their stroke. An actor on stage doesn't watch their hands as they gesture or listen to their voice as they speak their lines. The golfer and the actor want to lose themselves in their roles, not reflect on the mechanics of their performance.

So it is with us in our daily lives. When we turn the spotlight of attention on ourselves, we become self-conscious. What should be natural and spontaneous self-expression becomes an agonizing performance. *Spotlighting* makes you feel different and separate from others. Everything you say starts to sound odd or fake. You don't trust or like how you are coming across, and to make matters worse, you assume everyone else is watching you as closely as you are watching yourself. How can you get into the flow of life and connect with others when you are preoccupied with what is going on inside yourself?

Everyone feels self-conscious from time to time, but most people notice it happening and let it go. They flick a switch and turn the spotlight off. But when socially anxious teens feel self-conscious, they dial up the spotlight, increasing their self-consciousness to the point where they are paralyzed.

You can spotlight what is going on in your body as well. If you are sweating, shaking, or blushing, and you focus your attention on that, these normal signs of anxiety intensify. For example, when you are speaking in class you may notice that your heart is beating fast. Then, as you focus your attention on your heartbeat, the pounding intensifies until it feels like your heart might jump right out of your chest. "Everyone around me can see what's happening," you think to yourself. "They know I'm freaking out!" As you leave the room after class, the spotlight follows you, showing everybody how awkwardly you walk. And so it goes throughout the day when you are living in the spotlight.

Tell about a situation where you feel as if you are in the spotlight.

_____

_____

_____

_____

_____

How do you imagine you are coming across to others?

_____

_____

_____

What feelings do you have that you're sure people around you must see?

_____

_____

_____

Mind Reading

If you feel like you are in a spotlight and everyone is watching you, it's only natural for you to also worry that everyone is thinking about you. As a *mind reader*, you assume you know what people are thinking, especially when it is something bad about you. You haven't any psychic powers, but somehow you just know.

And because you are so certain, you don't bother to check out what is actually happening. For example, a friend told you she was going to meet you somewhere, but she didn't show up. Since you read her mind, you know it is because she thinks you are a loser, and the only reason she told you she would meet you was because she felt sorry for you. Your friend may have just forgotten, but instead of asking her about it, you say nothing.

Describe an interaction you had with someone that made you anxious.

_____

_____

_____

_____

_____

_____

What did you think they were thinking about you?

_____

_____

_____

Negative Comparisons

We all compare ourselves to others. When we get a grade on a paper, it is natural to want to know how others did on it as well. Sometimes these comparisons can inspire us, making us want to work harder to achieve our goals—for example, social media influencers may give you creative ideas of how to groom or dress. Seeing a skilled musician perform can motivate you to practice your own instrument more diligently.

But *negative comparisons*, where we choose only attractive, successful, or wealthy people to compare ourselves to, make us feel much worse about ourselves. If you compare yourself to a Super Bowl–winning quarterback, or even the star of your own high school team, how will this affect your confidence? Is it wise to restrict your calorie intake, trying to look like fashion models who represent a tiny percentage of the human population regarding weight and culturally desirable features, and are digitally enhanced as well? And how can you afford to purchase the kind of clothes, phones, or cars of those who are wealthier than you?

Winning social respect by matching others' looks, grades, possessions, or talents is a losing strategy because there will always be someone with more, requiring more effort from us to keep up. When we think we don't compare well, and have little chance of doing so, we may feel inadequate, grow depressed, and stop trying at all. While we can't help seeing others who have more of what we want, we are much more likely to feel badly when we negatively compare ourselves to them.

An Unconscious Belief

Disastrous distortions are not exclusively the domain of teens with social anxiety. If you pay attention to what your peers, your parents, even public figures say, you'll notice that everybody, socially anxious or not, catastrophizes, discounts the positive, labels, spotlights, mind reads, and negatively compares all the time. What makes these distorted thoughts such a big problem for socially anxious teens is when they are used alongside one more final distortion—I promise it's the last one! It's the most disastrous of them all, because it's more than a distorted thought. It's a distorted *belief*. Every socially anxious teen unconsciously believes that, *I can't afford to make a mistake.* This belief system is known as *social perfectionism,* and it's the subject of the next chapter.

Chapter 6

Social Perfectionism
The Path to Nowhere

Let's start this chapter with a social perfectionism quiz.

Social Perfectionism Quiz

Evaluate each of the following statements on a scale from 1 to 5, where 1 = disagree strongly and 5 = agree strongly.

_____ *If I tell a joke, it should be funny to everyone.*

_____ *If I don't get enough likes online, it means people don't like me.*

_____ *If there is an awkward silence in the conversation, it is probably my fault.*

_____ *If I stumble or stutter, people will think there's something wrong with me.*

_____ *If I say something that turns out to be wrong, people will think I'm stupid.*

_____ *If I don't text or post just the right thing, people will think I'm boring.*

_____ *If I forget people's names, they will think I don't care about them.*

_____ *If I wear something that somebody criticizes, I have bad taste in clothing.*

_____ *If I say something that someone takes the wrong way, I am insensitive.*

_____ *If I give an oral presentation, I should be relaxed and confident.*

_____ *If I appear nervous (for example, I blush or shake), others will see me as weak.*

How did your answers add up? Your total on this quiz isn't a scientific measurement, but generally speaking, the higher your score, the lower your allowance for making mistakes in social situations. Any effort you make to connect with others that isn't received with a 100 percent positive reaction is thought of as not good enough, unacceptable. This is *social perfectionism,* the belief system that shy and socially anxious teens all share.

I Can't Make Mistakes

Right now, you may be saying to yourself, "Those statements in that quiz don't sound like perfectionism, they sound realistic. Perfectionists are overachievers, people who work themselves to death getting A+s and winning first place. I'm not a perfectionist." While overachieving behavior may be the popular image of perfectionism, it is the *belief* that nothing less than an A+ or first place is acceptable that makes one a perfectionist. All socially anxious teens, to one degree or another, are social perfectionists. They don't allow themselves to risk making social errors, because they don't believe they could handle the criticism or rejection an error might cause.

It's pretty difficult to succeed as a social perfectionist. You must always be interesting, always be relaxed, always funny or smart or pretty, or whatever way you think you should be. You have a higher expectation for yourself than you do for everybody else, higher than you could possibly meet. For you, there is no such thing as being okay. You are never good enough.

Allowing no room for error is a ruthless way to judge yourself. This is why socially anxious teens so often suffer from low self-esteem. As long as your idea of acceptable is everyone approving of you all the time, you'll be unable to fully accept yourself. And you won't be willing to take the risks necessary to succeed in your goals.

Reality Check

Part of what makes it so difficult to question the belief that you can't make mistakes is that socially anxious teens perceive everybody else as not making any. (This is amplified by their tendency toward that disastrous distortion, negative comparison.) Are your peers as socially correct as you imagine they are? Do sports heroes, movie stars, and celebrities always get it right?

Think of someone you admire a lot. This could be someone in your family, a famous musician, an athletic hero, a media celebrity, or a historic figure. They are probably very talented and really good at something, but that does not make them good at everything. They also have flaws. They may have struggled with drugs, they may have done things that were not ethical, and they've definitely made mistakes. This is because no matter how famous or talented you are, you are still human. And human beings, every last one of us, are flawed.

The more you know about popular, successful people, the more imperfect they'll look. In fact, they often make *more* mistakes than the average person. What we admire about them isn't that they never make mistakes, it's that they are so clear about what they value in life that they are willing to risk making mistakes to live by those values.

When the most important thing you value is not making a social mistake, what does that say about your other personal values? When we overvalue staying safe from rejection in social situations, we are undervaluing something else. What are you undervaluing in your life?

Acting on Values

For many teens, identifying values is difficult. It's much easier to talk about goals, like getting an A on a test, winning a game, having a romance, getting a job, or being accepted to a university. Goals are what we want to get in life. Values are how we want to get there. Our goals define what we hope to achieve. Our values define the person trying to achieve them.

What do you value? Is it safety, not making mistakes, having everyone like you, never being rejected? When staying safe from criticism is our highest value, we don't try things that we are interested in. We don't pursue friends and activities because we are afraid others will see our flaws. Here are some other qualities that people value highly; circle those that appeal to you.

Fun	Spontaneity
Connection	Risk-taking
Growth	Adventure
Honesty	Creativity
Self-expression	Courage
Authenticity	Independence

Of the values you circled, which of them are you actually living by? If your ultimate goal is connection with others and belonging, you'll need to start living by your values to get there. Shared human values are the glue that secures the deepest bonds between people.

Remember Alex, whose goal is to meet Ginelle? The values he circled were courage and authenticity. If he tries to meet that goal without living by those values, something will be lost. For example, if he got a friend to ask Ginelle whether she was interested in him, he would not be living by his value of courage. Or, if instead of pursuing Ginelle, he pursues only girls he's not attracted to, who don't make him anxious, he would not be living authentically. Or, to put it a positive way, *If you act on your values, even if you do not meet your goal, you are succeeding.*

Recognizing values is especially important for Alex and for all socially anxious teens. If Alex honors his values of courage and authenticity by introducing himself to Ginelle, even if he can't think of anything to say that is clever enough to impress her, he is still moving forward. But in his scenario, rather than follow the direction that his values would take him, Alex is sidetracked on a path to nowhere.

He's acting as if the most important things in his life—what he most values—is that he never be the cause of an awkward silence in a conversation, that he never say anything that could be judged as weird. His primary value is safety, avoiding negative criticism. Without a higher value than staying safe, he is bound to repeat his own chain reaction, always ending in avoidance.

This next exercise will help you examine your goals and values in more detail. A copy of this worksheet is also available at http://www.new harbinger.com/48015.

Goals and Values Worksheet

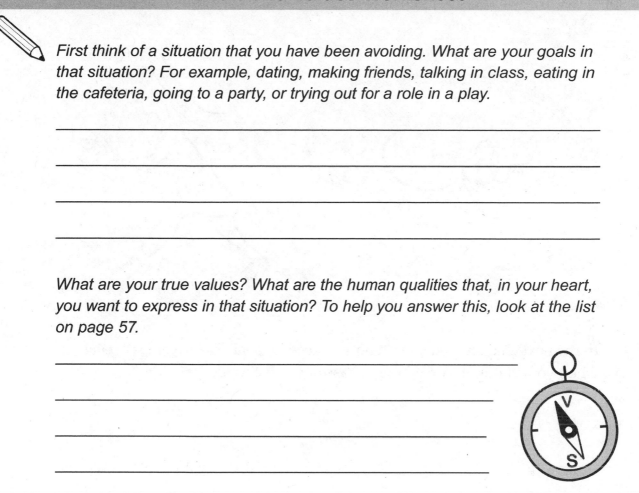

First think of a situation that you have been avoiding. What are your goals in that situation? For example, dating, making friends, talking in class, eating in the cafeteria, going to a party, or trying out for a role in a play.

_____

_____

_____

_____

What are your true values? What are the human qualities that, in your heart, you want to express in that situation? To help you answer this, look at the list on page 57.

_____

_____

_____

_____

Goals change over time, but your values can always act as a reliable compass in life. North is toward your values. South is toward safety and avoidance. As long as you follow your own true north—the qualities of character you know in your heart you value most—no reasonable goal is beyond your reach.

In the next chapter, you'll learn how to keep on a values-driven path even when your thoughts are getting disastrously distorted.

What Was I Thinking?

Chapter 7

Two Ways to Test Your Thoughts

If what we think determines how we feel, and how we feel guides our actions, then our thoughts, being the first link in the chain, play a pretty important role in our lives. Our success and happiness are riding on those thoughts, yet as we learned in the chapter on disastrous distortions, our thoughts, especially the automatic thoughts that pop up in triggering social situations, are not reliable and are open to interpretation.

On the next page let's look at how three different thoughts about this situation can spark three different sets of feelings and actions.

THOUGHT #1

I DON'T THINK SHE LIKES ME.

ANXIETY

DON'T TEXT FRIEND UNLESS THEY TEXT YOU.

THOUGHT #2

THAT WAS RUDE!

ANGER

DITCH YOUR PHONE AND YOUR FRIEND.

THOUGHT #3

SHE'S PROBABLY BUSY.

EMPATHY

TEXT FRIEND AGAIN A LITTLE LATER.

You may very well be wondering, "So how do I know which thought is correct?" That is a good question, and the answer is that you can't ever be certain that what you are thinking is accurate, especially when you're thinking about what other people are thinking! But you can take a closer look at them. Examining the automatic thoughts that drive your feelings and actions is an important first step in moving toward your goals.

Testing Automatic Thoughts

There are two ways to test a thought. The first way is to fact-check it; if you spot any disastrous distortions, your thought can't be trusted. The second way is to examine what that thought leads you to ultimately *do*. Does acting on that thought move you toward or away from your goals and values?

Let's evaluate the first two of Brandi's thoughts for reliability, looking at the entire thought-feeling-behavior chain that each of them sparked. Were they distorted? Did they move her to avoid the situation or toward her goal? Toward safety or more important personal values?

Automatic Thoughts	Distortions	Feelings	Behavior	Direction Avoidance or Goals & Values?
"She doesn't like me."	Mind reading, catastrophizing	Embarrassment, shame	Don't text until reassured	Avoidance
"That was rude!"	Labeling, discounting the positive	Anger, humiliation, disappointment	Cancel friend	Avoidance
"She's probably busy."			Text again later	Goals & values

Of the three thoughts, #3 is the only one that has no distortions. It also prompts Brandi to allow her text to go unanswered without judging her friend. If Brandi's goal is to maintain her relationship with her friend and she values loyalty and trust, thought #3 is the one that passes the test.

Here is Chris, checking his social media stream for responses to his posts without much luck. Follow along with the chart to see how different thoughts Chris might have could send him in different directions.

Automatic Thoughts	Distortions	Feelings	Behavior	Direction Avoidance or Goals & Values?
"People don't like me."	Mind reading, catastrophizing	Sadness, disappointment	Stop posting	Avoidance
"They think my posts are weird."	Labeling, mind reading	Embarrassment, shame, rapid heartbeat	Stop posting or **compulsively rework posts	Avoidance
"Maybe if I respond to others' posts, they'll respond more to mine."			Continue to post	Goals & values

Of these three thoughts, only the third moves Chris toward his goal of building connections on social media, as well as his most important personal value, which is to be authentic. This thought also passes the fact-check test; it's true that people are more likely to reach out to someone who has reached out to them first.

** Compulsively deleting and rewriting posts is a subtle form of avoidance called a *safety behavior*. You'll learn more about safety behaviors in chapter 11.

Let's do this exercise with Lucia, who thinks she's a boring conversationalist.

Automatic Thoughts	Distortions	Feelings	Behavior	Direction Avoidance or Goals & Values?
"I don't have anything to say."	Social perfectionism	Self-consciousness	Don't speak	Avoidance
"They're noticing how quiet I am."	Mind reading, spotlighting	Embarrassment	Wait for someone to speak to her	Avoidance
"They think I'm weird."	Labeling, catastrophizing	Shame	Withdraw completely	Avoidance

What does Lucia's withdrawal from the conversation tell us about the reliability of the thoughts that drove her behavior?

_____

_____

_____

_____

Can you think of a thought for Lucia that would pass a fact-check and values test?

_____

_____

_____

_____

Remember Bella, the girl introducing herself to a group?
Let's break her scenario down for her.

Automatic Thoughts	Distortions	Feelings	Behavior	Direction Avoidance or Goals & Values?
"When I talk, my face will turn red and my voice will crack."	Spotlighting, catastrophizing, social perfectionism	Anxiety, embarrassment	Lower head, say little to avoid being seen or heard	Avoidance
"Everyone will see how anxious I am."	Spotlighting, social perfectionism	Shame	Lower head, say little to avoid being seen or heard	Avoidance

Can you think of a thought for Bella in this situation that would pass a fact-check and values test?

_____

_____

_____

_____

_____

Take a look at a personal situation that makes you anxious. If you need ideas, go back to the chain reactions you filled in on page 29. The next worksheet will help you test your automatic thoughts. A copy of this worksheet is also available at http://www.newharbinger.com/48015.

The Automatic Thought Test

Situation	
Automatic Thoughts	
Distortions	☐ **Catastrophizing** (assuming the worst possible outcome) ☐ **Discounting the positive** (refusing to take credit when you deserve it) ☐ **Labeling** (putting a negative name on yourself) ☐ **Spotlighting** (thinking everybody is watching you and/or how you feel inside shows on the outside) ☐ **Mind reading** (guessing what others are thinking or will think) ☐ **Negative comparison** (comparing yourself to others who are popular or successful) ☐ **Social perfectionism** (the belief that mistakes are unacceptable)
Feelings	
Behavior	
Direction Avoidance or Goals & Values?	

You're on a roll; let's do a couple more.

Situation	
Automatic Thoughts	
Distortions	☐ **Catastrophizing** (assuming the worst possible outcome) ☐ **Discounting the positive** (refusing to take credit when you deserve it) ☐ **Labeling** (putting a negative name on yourself) ☐ **Spotlighting** (thinking everybody is watching you and/or how you feel inside shows on the outside) ☐ **Mind reading** (guessing what others are thinking or will think) ☐ **Negative comparison** (comparing yourself to others who are popular or successful) ☐ **Social perfectionism** (the belief that mistakes are unacceptable)
Feelings	
Behavior	
Direction Avoidance or Goals & Values?	

Situation	
Automatic Thoughts	
Distortions	☐ **Catastrophizing** (assuming the worst possible outcome) ☐ **Discounting the positive** (refusing to take credit when you deserve it) ☐ **Labeling** (putting a negative name on yourself) ☐ **Spotlighting** (thinking everybody is watching you and/or how you feel inside shows on the outside) ☐ **Mind reading** (guessing what others are thinking or will think) ☐ **Negative comparison** (comparing yourself to others who are popular or successful) ☐ **Social perfectionism** (the belief that mistakes are unacceptable)
Feelings	
Behavior	
Direction Avoidance or Goals & Values?	

By now you are probably thinking, "Okay, I get the point. My automatic thoughts are distorted, and they are making me do stuff that isn't helping me move toward my goals and values. But I can't just block them out, can I? I can't simply *not* think them!"

You can't stop yourself from thinking automatic thoughts. They're automatic. But you can come up with alternative ways to think. The next chapter will show you how.

Chapter 8

Talking Back to Your Thoughts

Training Your Brain to Challenge and Cope

Ever try not to think of a banana? It doesn't have to be a banana—it could be any word—but for argument's sake, let's try it with "banana." For the next thirty seconds, don't think about a banana. 1...2...3...4...

...27...28...29...30.

Did you succeed? Probably not. Trying to push thoughts out of our minds won't get rid of them; in fact, it can make them worse. What we can do is question them.

Challenge Questions

Questioning what we're thinking is the first step to changing our minds. As a socially anxious teen, you'll have plenty of disastrous distortions to question. Whenever a thought comes up that stands in the way of reaching your goals and living according to your values, address it with a *challenge question*.

What challenge questions might Alex have asked himself when Ginelle appeared?

Alex's automatic thought: I won't know what to say.

Distortion: Social perfectionism

His challenge question: Is it OK to just smile and say hi? Do I know for certain that I won't have anything to say?

Alex's automatic thought: Ginelle will think I'm weird.

Distortion: Labeling

Challenge question: Does not saying something clever equal being weird?

That thought had a couple of distortions, so let's do it again.

Alex's automatic thought: Ginelle will think I'm weird.

Distortion: Mind reading

His challenge question: Do I know for certain what Ginelle will think?

Alex's automatic thought: If I embarrass myself in front of her, she will talk to all her friends about how weird I am, and then the whole school will think I am weird.

Distortion: Catastrophizing

His challenge question: What is more likely to happen? How could I cope with that?

And after the experience…

Alex's automatic thought: She barely recognized me. All she did was say hi.

Distortion: Discounting the positive

His challenge question: What did I do that was okay?

Coping Thoughts

Challenge questions aren't hypothetical; they deserve an answer. The answers to challenge questions become your *coping thoughts*. Let's see what coping thoughts Alex came up with.

Alex's challenge question: Is it OK to just smile and say hi? Do I know for certain that I won't have anything to say?

His coping thoughts: I might be able to think of something to say. I'm pretty sure I can smile and say hi. That's something.

Alex's challenge question: Does not saying something clever equal being weird?

His coping thoughts: When other people don't know what to say, I don't think they're weird. Ginelle may not think I'm weird either.

Alex's challenge question: What is more likely to happen? How could I cope with that?

His coping thoughts: It is unlikely that the whole school would know I talked to Ginelle. It is more likely that she doesn't even look at me. She could act all rude and stuck up. If that happened, I could talk it over with a friend and at least I would know she's not for me.

And after the experience ...

Alex's challenge question: What did I do that was okay?

His coping thoughts: I was assertive. I walked right up to her and said hi. I proved to myself that I'm braver than I thought. Now she knows I exist and I have a chance of getting to know her better.

Now it's your turn to create challenge questions and coping thoughts for your own anxiety-producing scenarios. A copy of this worksheet is also available at http://www.newharbinger.com/48015.

Create Challenge Questions and Coping Thoughts

Fill in the following chart based on one of your own anxious thoughts. Feel free to use these challenge questions:

- **Catastrophizing:** *What is more likely to happen? How could I cope with that?*
- **Discounting the positive:** *What did I do that was okay?*
- **Labeling:** *Does this word apply to me all the time in every situation?*
- **Spotlighting:** *What else might everyone be paying attention to besides me? Do people really care that much about what I am doing?*
- **Mind reading:** *What evidence do I have that this is what people are thinking?*
- **Negative comparison:** *Am I comparing myself to others in a way that makes me feel worse about myself?*
- **Social perfectionism:** *Am I asking more of myself than I would of others?*

Anxious Thoughts	
Distortions	☐ **Catastrophizing** (assuming the worst possible outcome) ☐ **Discounting the positive** (refusing to take credit when you deserve it) ☐ **Labeling** (putting a negative name on yourself) ☐ **Spotlighting** (thinking everybody is watching you and/or how you feel inside shows on the outside) ☐ **Mind reading** (guessing what others are thinking or will think) ☐ **Negative comparison** (comparing yourself to others who are popular or successful) ☐ **Social perfectionism** (the belief that mistakes are unacceptable)
Challenge Question	
Coping Thought	

Having an alternative to the distorted automatic thoughts you've been using for so long is a fundamental tool in the battle to overcome social anxiety. Coping thoughts will help you face the situations you've been avoiding and move toward your goals and values. Every time you choose to act on a coping thought rather than on an anxious automatic thought, you help create a new chain of thinking, feeling, and behaving.

Having a more realistic idea of the threat of being judged and rejected is great. But when you start moving toward what you want in life, there is always the possibility that you *will* be judged and rejected. In the next chapter, you'll learn the tools you'll need to cope with that too.

Chapter 9

To the Rescue!

*Coping with Criticism—
Real, Imagined, and
Self-Inflicted*

Being judged or criticized is always a
possibility in any social interaction. It happens
to everybody, whether face to face or on social
media, where comments can be made more
impulsively as well as more public. Getting
fewer likes than others can feel like criticism too.

But as we have learned, socially anxious teens
overestimate the threat that criticism directed
at them will lead to rejection—being kicked out
of their tribe. And because they avoid situations
where they may be criticized, they don't learn
how to cope with it when it happens. Yet if we want to be connected with
others, whether we are online or face to face, we need to be able to cope with
occasional criticism.

What do I mean by "cope"? Does coping mean "putting up with" or
"suffering through"? No, coping is not a passive behavior; it's a decidedly
active one. It means being assertive, standing up for yourself, and coming to
your own rescue. This chapter will teach you how to do exactly that.

Coping skills will take some practice to master, but we're not going to wait
until someone criticizes you to begin practicing. We'd have to wait too long,
because real criticism, where someone actually says something negative
about you, is the rarest type of criticism we face. Much more common is
the criticism that you experience inside your own head. Unable to know for
certain what others are thinking, socially anxious teens imagine the worst,
that others are watching everything they do with a critical eye. To make
matters worse, long after their social interactions are over, socially anxious
teens often heap criticism on themselves, replaying what they said or did
over and over, beating themselves up for their mistakes.

Fortunately, you can learn how to cope with all three types of criticism: the real kind, the imagined kind, and the kind you inflict on yourself. The following exercise will show you how. Before you try it yourself, let's walk through it with Lucia and Brandi.

Lucia

Lucia thinks that she should sound interesting and smart when she talks to people—social perfectionism. She often avoids conversations, worried that others will think she is boring. When she does get up the courage to talk with someone, afterward she obsesses about the possibility that the other person was bored with her and doesn't want to be her friend. To feel confident joining conversations, Lucia wanted to feel like she can handle being criticized by others. But because she couldn't think of a time when someone actually told her she was boring, for this exercise she used a situation where she imagined she was being criticized—mind reading.

Lucia was beating herself up for trying to start a conversation with Sara from her English class, asking her if she had finished the book report that was due that Friday. Sara answered "yes," without saying anything else. Lucia imagined that Sara didn't continue the conversation because she found Lucia to be boring.

Example: Lucia's Coping with Criticism Worksheet

1. First, Lucia thinks of a situation where she was, or might be, criticized—in this case, imagining that Sara thinks she is boring.

   Situation: Asking Sara about the book report in class.

2. Next, she writes down the worst thing she imagined Sara was thinking about her.

   Criticism: I don't know why you're asking me about the book report, don't you have anything interesting to talk about?

3. Lucia needs to think up an assertive response. She does not need to convince Sara that she is not boring. "Assertive" means standing up for herself without getting defensive or aggressive.

   Assertive response: That may not have been the most interesting topic to you, but it was all I could think of. I'm just trying to be friendly and get to know you.

4. That's a good start. Now Lucia imagines the worst thing that Sara might think or say to respond to her response.

   New criticism: Well, I don't want to be friends with someone who asks me boring, stupid questions.

5. Once again, Lucia replies assertively.

   Assertive response: You're entitled to your opinion. I think asking a boring question is better than not saying anything.

6. Again, Lucia imagines the worst thing that Sara might think or say to her response.

   New criticism: You're boring and I don't want to be your friend.

7. And again, Lucia replies assertively.

   Assertive response: Okay. I don't want to be your friend if you feel this way. I'm still proud of myself for being friendly.

After doing the exercise, Lucia felt a bit a less anxious about the possibility that Sara *was* judging her that day. If Sara really was that judgmental, Lucia realized, she wouldn't want her as a friend. She stopped kicking herself for trying to start the conversation, and started patting herself on the back for being brave and moving toward her values of connection and her goal of making new friends. She moved from catastrophizing, to coping. And now Lucia also feels a little bit more confident about future conversations where others might judge her negatively.

Brandi

Let's go through the exercise now with Brandi. She shared a selfie on social media and just as she feared, someone, her friend Janine, tagged it with a snarky comment. Let's look at how Brandi did with this coping exercise.

Example: Brandi's Coping with Criticism Worksheet

1. First, Brandi writes down a description of the situation on the worksheet.

    Situation: Posted a selfie and got a snarky comment from Janine.

2. Next, she writes down the critical thing the person said.

    Criticism: "Bad hair day????"

3. Brandi needs to think up an assertive response. She does not need to convince Janine that her photo is good. "Assertive" means standing up for herself without getting defensive or aggressive.

    Assertive response: I think my hair looks okay in this picture.

4. Next, Brandi imagines the worst thing that Janine might say to her response.

    New criticism: It looks messy.

5. Once again, Brandi replies assertively.

    Assertive response: That's my style. I like it wild.

6. Again, Brandi imagines the worst thing that Janine might think or say to her response.

    New criticism: Well it doesn't look good that way.

7. And again, Brandi replies assertively.

    Assertive response: I like it even if you don't.

Get the idea? Now it is your turn. Think of a
social situation where you are afraid you may be
judged or criticized by someone. Or, like Brandi,
you could pick a situation where someone did
actually say something judgmental.

While you could do this exercise entirely in your
head, you'll get a better workout if you write
the conversation down. Then you can either
find someone to role-play the critic or, since we
are usually our own worst critic, you can easily
play both roles in the exchange. A copy of this
worksheet is also available at http://www
.newharbinger.com/48015.

Coping with Criticism Worksheet

1. Anxiety-triggering social situation:

   _____

2. What are you afraid that others might think or say about you?

   _____

   _____

   _____

3. If someone did say or do something that was critical, what would be an assertive response?

   _____

   _____

   _____

4. Imagine the criticism persists. What would they say?

   _____

   _____

   _____

5. Come up with another assertive response you can make.

_____

_____

_____

6. What would the critic say?

_____

_____

_____

7. How can you continue to stand up for yourself?

_____

_____

_____

The more often you practice coping exercises on paper, the better you will get at standing up for yourself when you need to. Remember that whenever criticism happens to you, whether the real kind or what you imagine, you always have a choice. You can kick yourself in the pants or you can pat yourself on the back. Which will you do?

With that in mind, read on! In the next chapter you're going to learn the best way to practice applying everything you've learned thus far, without being overwhelmed.

Chapter 10   # Building the Ladder
From Avoidance to Action

Let's return to our friend Alex. He's done some good work defining his values, and he understands how avoiding scary situations takes him further from getting what he wants. He's identified the automatic thoughts that drive his anxious feelings and avoidance behavior, and he's examined those thoughts for distortions, posed challenge questions, and come up with coping thoughts. He should be okay now, right? Shouldn't his avoidance behavior pretty well have disappeared for him, and for you too, if you've been doing the work in this book?

Not so fast. Coping thoughts won't simply replace your distorted anxious thoughts. Like vampires, these thoughts will live forever unless they are exposed to sunlight. To really change the way we think, we need exposure to the very social situations we've been avoiding, where negative judgments from others can actually happen, and we can practice coping with them. For Alex to gain confidence in himself, he's going to have to actually talk to Ginelle. Alex needs to turn his avoidance situation into an *exposure* situation.

Exposure Ideas Worksheet

Take a moment to choose your own avoidance situation to transform into an exposure. Consider each situation on the following chart. Rate it for scariness, and check the box that, given your goals and values, best indicates how important each situation is for you. At the bottom of the list are some blank lines where you can write situations of your own.

Avoidance Situation	How Scary 1–3 1 = Not So Scary 3 = Very Scary	How Important 1–3 1 = Not So Important 3 = Very Important
Starting or joining a conversation		
Answering questions in class		
Inviting a friend to get together		
Taking a test		
Initiating a text to someone you don't know well		
Entering a room where others are already seated		
Writing on the whiteboard or chalkboard		
Posting comments or photos on social media		
Working with a group of teens		
Participating in P.E. class		

Creating a social media profile		
Walking in the hallways or hanging out by your locker		
Asking a teacher a question or for help		
Responding to a text someone sent you		
Using school or public bathrooms		
Eating in front of others		
Writing in front of others		
Answering or talking on the phone		
Performing in public		
Giving a report or reading aloud in front of the class		
Speaking to adults (for example, store clerks, waiters, or your principal)		
Talking to new or unfamiliar people		
Attending parties, dances, or school activity nights		
Having your picture taken (for example, for your school yearbook)		
Dating		

Now that you've identified which of the situations you've been avoiding are most important to you, let's pick one to begin working on. It should be a situation that reflects your values. You are going to turn that avoidance situation into an exposure.

Don't worry, nobody's going to push you off the exposure high dive. You're going to build your own personal ladder to the top, an *exposure ladder,* with manageable steps you can climb at your own pace.

The Exposure Ladder

To help us get a handle on how an exposure ladder works, let's look at what Alex created for himself. His goal was to ask Ginelle out on a date, which he rated a 10 in scariness. Exposing himself to that level of embarrassment seemed an impossible goal, certainly not something he could accomplish all at once. Alex put asking Ginelle for a date at the very top of his ladder, with rungs of smaller, less scary steps leading up to it.

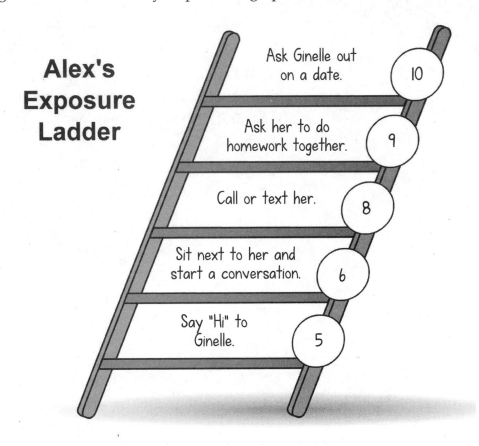

Alex's Exposure Ladder

Ask Ginelle out on a date. — 10

Ask her to do homework together. — 9

Call or text her. — 8

Sit next to her and start a conversation. — 6

Say "Hi" to Ginelle. — 5

Here are several sample ladders built for common avoidance/exposure situations. The order of the rungs would probably be different for each person completing the ladder. Rate how scary each exposure would be for you by putting a number from 1 to 10 in the circle.

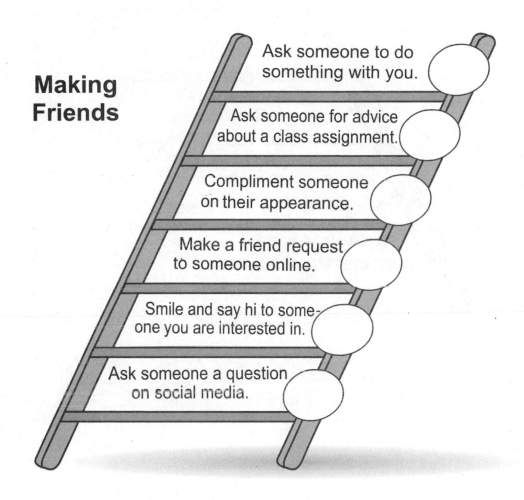

Making Friends

Ask someone to do something with you.

Ask someone for advice about a class assignment.

Compliment someone on their appearance.

Make a friend request to someone online.

Smile and say hi to someone you are interested in.

Ask someone a question on social media.

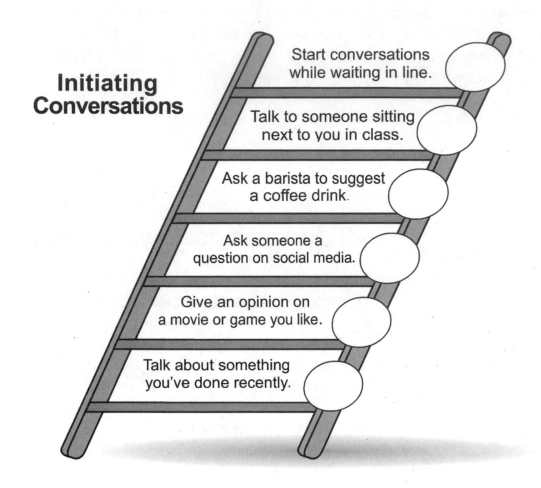

Initiating Conversations

Start conversations while waiting in line.

Talk to someone sitting next to you in class.

Ask a barista to suggest a coffee drink.

Ask someone a question on social media.

Give an opinion on a movie or game you like.

Talk about something you've done recently.

Dating

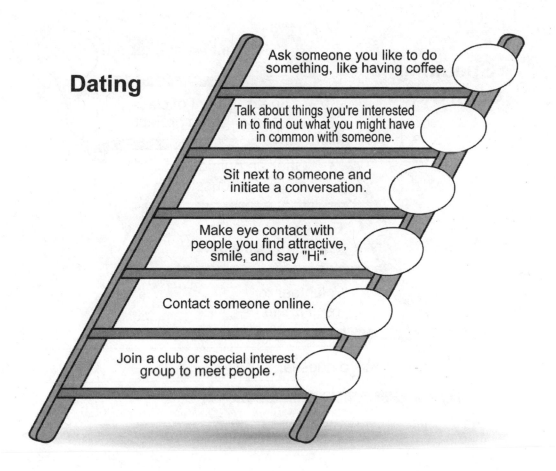

Ask someone you like to do something, like having coffee.

Talk about things you're interested in to find out what you might have in common with someone.

Sit next to someone and initiate a conversation.

Make eye contact with people you find attractive, smile, and say "Hi".

Contact someone online.

Join a club or special interest group to meet people.

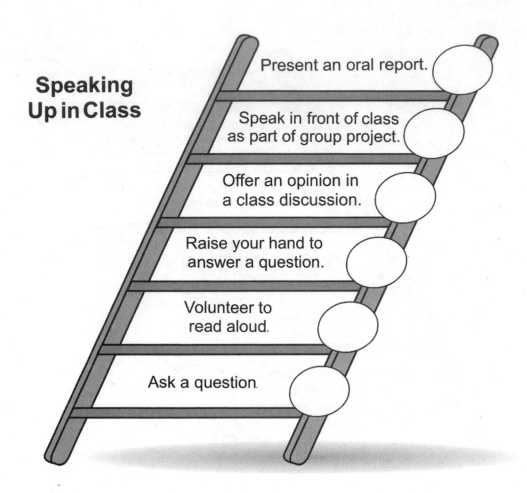

Speaking Up in Class

Present an oral report.

Speak in front of class as part of group project.

Offer an opinion in a class discussion.

Raise your hand to answer a question.

Volunteer to read aloud.

Ask a question.

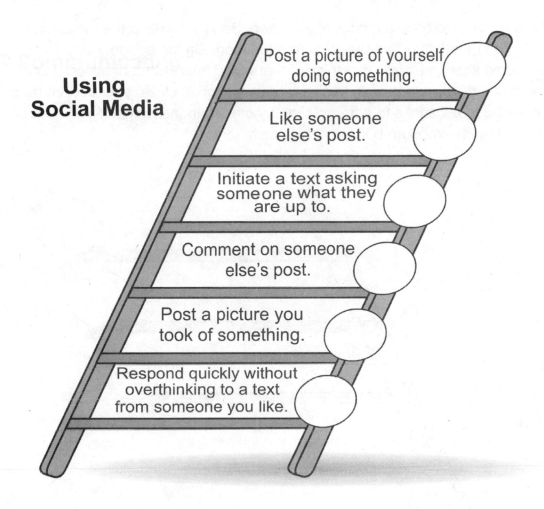

Using Social Media

Post a picture of yourself doing something.

Like someone else's post.

Initiate a text asking someone what they are up to.

Comment on someone else's post.

Post a picture you took of something.

Respond quickly without overthinking to a text from someone you like.

This next exercise will help you create your own exposure ladder. A copy of this worksheet is also available at http://www.newharbinger.com/48015.

Now it's time to build a ladder of your own. Begin by writing the avoidance situation most important to you on the top rung. On the bottom rung, write the least scary step you can think of that would lead in that direction. For example, if your top rung is to give a presentation in class, your bottom rung might be to tell a joke to a friend. One by one, fill in the rungs of your ladder so that each exposure builds on the one before.

Keep your exposure ladder handy; you're going to need it for the next chapter, where you'll learn how to go from building your ladder to actually climbing it!

Chapter 11 ## Charting Success

Preparing for and Evaluating Exposures

Have you completed your exposure ladder? Great—good work! You're almost ready to start your climb.

Chances are, you're not exactly jumping at the opportunity to do your first exposure; you may have tried something similar in the past and regretted it. But this time, you're going to have a new strategy and a more accurate way to evaluate your results. And you'll have a powerful support tool to help you execute that strategy and your evaluation. It's called an *exposure chart*.

The Exposure Chart

An exposure chart has two main parts. The first is the *pre-exposure*, which defines the social perfectionist way of thinking that has led to avoidance of this situation in the past, and outlines a new strategy moving forward. You've probably heard the saying, "Success is 90 percent preparation, and 10 percent perspiration." It's especially true for your success overcoming social anxiety. And the more anxious you are about an exposure, the more crucial it is to prepare with this chart.

The second part of the exposure chart is the *post-exposure*. This is to be filled out afterward to help you evaluate how you did. You'll most likely do better than you think you did, and the post-exposure will help you get an accurate view.

To understand how filling out an exposure chart will help you master a social situation, let's follow along with Alex as he charts his strategy to introduce himself to Ginelle.

Pre-Exposure Preparation

Alex begins by naming the *exposure* he's chosen, the lowest rung on his ladder. In the second field, he writes down his *perfectionist goal,* the unrealistic expectation he's placed on himself in the past when he's around Ginelle. Social perfectionism allows no room for mistakes or surprises, and if Alex tries this exposure believing he must stay calm and confident in order to succeed, he'll be destined to fail.

Next is Alex's *anxious prediction*—what he is afraid will happen (and probably feels absolutely certain will happen) when he approaches Ginelle. Alex's anxious predictions are based on one or more of the *disastrous distortions* we've learned about. They are listed in the next field, and Alex checks three that apply.

Example: Alex's Pre-Exposure Chart, Part A

Exposure	*What feared situation are you facing?* Saying hi to Ginelle
Perfectionist Goal	*How do you think you should act and appear in this situation?* Calm and confident
Anxious Prediction	*What are you afraid will happen?* I'll look nervous. She'll think I'm weird or creepy.
Distortions	*What distorted thinking does your anxious prediction rely on?* ☐ Catastrophizing (assuming the worst possible outcome) ☑ Discounting the positive (refusing to take credit when you deserve it) ☑ Labeling (putting a negative name on yourself) ☐ Spotlighting (thinking everybody is watching you and/or how you feel inside shows on the outside) ☑ Mind reading (guessing what others are thinking or will think) ☐ Negative comparison (comparing yourself to others who are popular or successful) ☑ Social perfectionism (the belief that mistakes are unacceptable)
Safety Behavior	*What would you normally do to prevent your anxious prediction from happening?*

This first section of his pre-exposure chart is nearly complete; there is just one more important question he must answer: *Whenever Alex was in close proximity to Ginelle, in the past, what did he do to keep himself from looking nervous and being judged by her?*

Alex had to think about that. He remembered sitting near Ginelle in a class the year before. He even said a few words to her briefly in a discussion about a quiz she and some other students in their part of the room were having, but before he opened his mouth, he mentally rehearsed what he was going to say so it wouldn't sound dumb. He never looked directly at Ginelle, and he spoke only about the quiz, not about anything personal. The moment he finished his rehearsed words and the conversation became spontaneous, Alex froze. He fixed his eyes on the floor and waited until the group broke up and the crisis had passed.

What Alex did is called *safety behavior,* and it is another, more subtle form of avoidance. Safety behaviors are what we do to keep the things we are afraid will happen from happening. It's like swimming with water wings on to keep yourself from drowning. Yes, you are in the water, but you're not really swimming. Wearing water wings help you gain confidence in water wings, not in your own ability to stay afloat.

Here are some examples of safety behaviors:

- *Calling a friend but planning what you are going to say first*

- *Going to a party, but not initiating conversations*

- *Asking someone out, but not the person you are really interested in*

- *Rewriting texts, posts, or comments to get them just right*

- *Going to school, but avoiding looking people in the eye*

- *Talking only to people who do not intimidate you*

- *Sitting in the back of the class so people cannot watch you*

- *Using alcohol or other drugs at social gatherings*

- *Never ordering things at restaurants that you are afraid you will mispronounce*

- *Spending a long time getting a photo just right to share on social media*

Alex knows from past experience that when he is around girls that he's attracted to, he avoids eye contact and never says anything that he hasn't rehearsed first in his head. If he does that now with Ginelle, he won't be exposing himself to what he's afraid of, his anxious prediction. Writing down the safety behavior he's used in the past will help him remember what not to do.

Safety Behavior	What would you normally do to prevent your anxious prediction from happening?
	Avoid eye contact, rehearse what I'm going to say

At this point, Alex has outlined the strategy that's kept him avoiding Ginelle. The second part of the chart is where Alex will outline the new strategy that will help him meet her. The first field asks what *realistic goal* Alex will set for himself, to replace his old perfectionist goal. His realistic goal should be clearly defined, something he can accomplish even though he may look nervous while accomplishing it. (Note: The realistic goal should not allow safety behavior!) If Alex walks up to Ginelle and says hi, no matter how she reacts or responds, Alex gets an A+.

This will likely trigger distorted thoughts and lots of anxiety, which brings us to the next field, Alex's *coping thought*. A coping thought is a combination of challenging our distorted thoughts and standing up for ourselves. Alex's coping thought will help give him courage to keep moving toward his goal to greet Ginelle.

Finally, Alex must answer the most important question he can ask himself, *What personal value is driving me in this direction?* He'll need to have that ready in his mind when the going gets rough; it is the compass that will keep him on course.

Realistic Goal	*What can you accomplish even though you feel anxious?* Smiling, looking her in the eye, trying to start a conversation
Coping Thought	*What can you remind yourself of when you are feeling the most anxious?* I am just being friendly. If she reacts negatively to me, I can cope with that. She may not even be the girl for me.
Values	*What motivates you to move in this direction?* Growth (Connection) Honesty (Self-Expression) Fun Authenticity Spontaneity Risk Adventure Creativity Independence (Courage)

This completes the pre-exposure part of the chart. Alex is now fully prepared for his exposure.

Doing the Exposure

As the moment he has chosen to approach Ginelle grows near, predictably, Alex's anxious thoughts intensify. His heart is beating faster, his face is getting hot, his muscles are tensing, and his hands are shaking. His mind is telling him not to do it, that he won't have anything to say and she will think he is an idiot. It will be obvious to Ginelle how nervous he is, he thinks, and she'll see him as weak and weird. If he listens to his thoughts right now, he'll stick his head in the locker.

If Alex is going to go through with this exposure, he's going to have to do it with the same old drumbeat of anxious thoughts that have been playing in his head for years every time an attractive girl is around. He's sick of that soundtrack, but when it's blasting away it makes him feel anxious, and when he feels anxious, his feet move him away from his goals and values.

The bottom line is that Alex will have to decide which drumbeat to dance to—that of his goals and values or that of his anxiety. He won't move toward his values if he gives his attention to his automatic thoughts and anxious feelings In life, as well as in sports, we win by keeping our eyes and ears on the prize.

Post-Exposure Evaluation

Well, that was awkward! Alex is both exhilarated and relieved. We might be wondering, was it worth it? Ginelle didn't smile brightly and fall in love with Alex on the spot. She couldn't even remember his name. Alex isn't really sure what she thinks about him now; she might even be laughing at him. Would Alex have been better off simply avoiding all that preparation and pain?

After any social interaction, and certainly after an exposure like Alex's, shy people often have doubts about themselves, obsessing about what they may have done wrong. Thoughts like "I should have said..." and "Why didn't I...?" echo in their heads. Replaying what they should have done is more perfectionist thinking. Nobody can meet that standard, and if Alex evaluates his experience on those terms he'll feel like a failure and go back to avoiding Ginelle.

The important things for Alex to ask himself are "Did I meet my realistic goal?" and "Did I move toward my values?" And the answer is yes to both questions. To help him appreciate what he accomplished and interrupt his "woulda, shoulda, coulda" thinking, Alex filled out his post-exposure chart.

Example: Alex's Post-Exposure Chart

Did I meet my realistic goal? How?	Yes. I walked up to Ginelle, smiled, and said hi.
Did I use safety behaviors? What did I do instead?	No. I spoke clearly and looked her straight in the eye.
How did I move toward my values?	I was friendly and I was true to myself.
What was the actual outcome?	Ginelle knows my name now. She knows that I am friendly and that I am interested in her.
What have I learned?	I said hi and it wasn't as bad as I thought it might be, and not as good as I had hoped, but okay and I am glad I did it.

Alex is in the pool now, up to about his ankles. This may seem like a small step, but it is an important one and it sure beats watching longingly from the deck. Ginelle may or may not remember him next time their paths cross, but if he continues using his values compass he will get to know her better. He might become her friend, or he might find out that Ginelle really isn't his type and wind up pursuing other girls instead. Either way, Alex's world is opening up. It won't be perfect; he'll certainly make mistakes, and he'll probably have to tolerate lots of anxious thoughts and feelings, but it is a slightly bigger, more interesting world to live in now. Your world can be expanded too. Are you ready to act on what is important to you and move ahead toward your values?

On the next page are blank pre- and post-exposure charts for you. Start with the least scary aspect of your avoidance situation, preferably one with a fear factor of less than 5. And remember that even though this is the lowest rung on your ladder, it should be treated as seriously as if it were the highest. Think carefully about each and every field in the chart. Just like a ladder, each step of the chart helps prepares you for the next one.

When you're finished with the pre-exposure section, commit yourself to a date and time. Then follow through with the exposure. Don't let the chatter of your monkey mind distract you. And don't forget to follow up with the post-exposure chart that's waiting for you! A copy of these worksheets is also available at http://www.newharbinger.com/48015.

Pre-Exposure Chart, Part A

Exposure	*What feared situation are you facing?*
Perfectionist Goal	*How do you think you should act and appear in this situation?*
Anxious Prediction	*What are you afraid will happen?*
Distortions	*What distorted thinking does your anxious prediction rely on?* ☐ Catastrophizing (assuming the worst possible outcome) ☐ Discounting the positive (refusing to take credit when you deserve it) ☐ Labeling (putting a negative name on yourself) ☐ Spotlighting (thinking everybody is watching you and/or how you feel inside shows on the outside) ☐ Mind reading (guessing what others are thinking or will think) ☐ Negative comparison (comparing yourself to others who are popular or successful) ☐ Social perfectionism (the belief that mistakes are unacceptable)
Safety Behavior	*What would you normally do to prevent your anxious prediction from happening?*

Pre-Exposure Chart, Part B

Realistic Goal	*What can you accomplish even though you feel anxious?*
Coping Thought	*What can you remind yourself of when you are feeling the most anxious?*
Values	*What motivates you to move in this direction?*

Under Values:

Growth	Connection	Honesty	Self-Expression
Fun	Authenticity	Spontaneity	Risk
Adventure	Creativity	Independence	Courage

Exposure Date: _____ Time: _____

Post-Exposure Chart

Did I meet my realistic goal? How?	
Did I use safety behaviors? What did I do instead?	
How did I move toward my values?	
What was the actual outcome?	
What have I learned?	

Don't continue this workbook until you've done your first exposure. In the next chapter, we're going to show you how each step on the ladder makes the next step possible!

Chapter 12

Bella's Ladder
Exposure, Exposure, Exposure

Now that you've started doing exposures, you are on a new path, headed in an unfamiliar direction. You will need to consult your values compass often. There will be new, more challenging situations around every bend, and tempting avoidance detours that promise to quiet your fears. To continue moving forward and meeting your goals, you will need to repeat the exposure process over and over. The good news is that every exposure, if done correctly, builds insight and confidence, making it possible to live a life according to your values.

Bella

To help you understand how repeated exposures move you up the ladder, let's follow Bella as she climbs hers. Bella started off by choosing something from the master list of avoidance situations in chapter 1—in her case, situations where people would see her blushing. This avoidance has been a problem for her because it has gotten in the way of answering or asking questions in class, talking to her friends, and applying for jobs. And those things were all consistent with her values, which were to share more of herself and be known by others, to go to college (she'd need to participate in class to get better grades), and to be more independent.

Bella decided that interviewing for a summer job, which represented her value for independence, would be a great goal. Since it was also the scariest thing she could think of, she put it at the top of her ladder. Then she worked her way down the rungs, listing less and less scary exposures she could do to move toward her goal.

Bella's Exposure Ladder

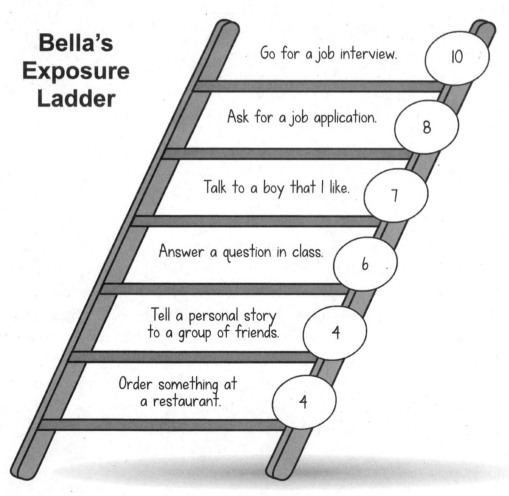

Go for a job interview. 10

Ask for a job application. 8

Talk to a boy that I like. 7

Answer a question in class. 6

Tell a personal story to a group of friends. 4

Order something at a restaurant. 4

Since she had no money for eating out, the lowest rung on her ladder, Bella decided to start out by telling a personal story to a group of her friends. Some funny things had happened when she went for her driver's test the previous weekend. The story would be easy to tell everyone in a text or online, but she had some very anxious thoughts about doing it face-to-face. She knew she'd blush and her friends would know how anxious she was, and make a big deal about it.

Bella was pretty sure her anxious thoughts were accurate, but she'd been dying to tell someone the story, so she asked herself, "If those things happen, what will I do?" To help herself answer that question, she completed a pre-exposure chart.

Exposure	*What feared situation are you facing?* Telling my friends a funny story face-to-face
Anxious Prediction	*What are you afraid will happen?* Everybody will judge me for looking anxious.
Distortions	*What distorted thinking does your anxious prediction rely on?* ☐ Catastrophizing (assuming the worst possible outcome) ☐ Discounting the positive (refusing to take credit when you deserve it) ☐ Labeling (putting a negative name on yourself) ☑ Spotlighting (thinking everybody is watching you and/or how you feel inside shows on the outside) ☑ Mind reading (guessing what others are thinking or will think) ☐ Negative comparison (comparing yourself to others who are popular or successful) ☑ Social perfectionism (the belief that mistakes are unacceptable)
Safety Behavior	*What would you normally do to prevent your anxious prediction from happening?* Don't blush or show any signs of anxiety.

Realistic Goal	*What can you accomplish even though you feel anxious?*
	Telling the story without stopping or resorting to safety behaviors
Coping Thought	*What can you remind yourself of when you are feeling the most anxious?*
	It's okay if I get anxious and blush; I can't stop that from happening.
Values	*What motivates you to move in this direction?*

Growth	(Connection)	Honesty	(Self-Expression)
Fun	(Authenticity)	Spontaneity	Risk
Adventure	Creativity	Independence	(Courage)

She set her exposure date for the next day after school. When the moment arrived, and she had a suitable audience, despite feeling the heat rise to her face, Bella plunged ahead. She swallowed hard, cleared her throat, and said, "You guys wanna hear what happened at my driver's test?"

Bella was right about one thing. She definitely blushed. But her predictions of her friends' reactions were off. Here's what her post-exposure chart looked like.

Did I meet my realistic goal? How?	Yes. I told the story.
Did I use safety behaviors? What did I do instead?	No. I wore just a little makeup and kept my hands away from my face.
How did I move toward my values?	I shared something personal and my friends all know me a little better.
What was the actual outcome?	I did blush and they did notice, but their reactions were friendly, not judgmental.
What have I learned?	My friends seem to accept the fact that I blush.

The next rung on Bella's ladder was to test the danger of blushing in front of a bigger group by raising her hand and answering a question in class. Although she often knew the answers, Bella never raised her hand; in fact, she sat in the back row and angled herself out of the teachers' lines of vision to avoid being called upon. She was certain that if she spoke in class everyone would look at her and notice her crimson face. Her last exposure had gone well, but it didn't give her enough courage for this. "After all," she thought, "they were my friends. I'm sure I won't get that kind of slack from my algebra class."

Bella's mind was reeling. Writing it all down in the chart really helped her organize her thoughts.

Example: Bella's Pre-Exposure Chart, Part A

Exposure	*What feared situation are you facing?* Raising my hand to answer a question in class
Perfectionist Goal	I can't let them see that I'm scared.
Anxious Prediction	*What are you afraid will happen?* I'll blush and the class will think I'm pathetic.
Distortions	*What distorted thinking does your anxious prediction rely on?* ☑ Catastrophizing (assuming the worst possible outcome) ☑ Discounting the positive (refusing to take credit when you deserve it) ☑ Labeling (putting a negative name on yourself) ☑ Spotlighting (thinking everybody is watching you and/or how you feel inside shows on the outside) ☑ Mind reading (guessing what others are thinking or will think) ☐ Negative comparison (comparing yourself to others who are popular or successful) ☑ Social perfectionism (the belief that mistakes are unacceptable)
Safety Behavior	*What would you normally do to prevent your anxious prediction from happening?* Lower my head and pull up my collar.

Realistic Goal	*What can you accomplish even though you feel anxious?* Raise my hand and answer the question.
Coping Thought	*What can you remind yourself of when you are feeling the most anxious?* If kids are mean or judgmental, it says more about them than about me.
Values	*What motivates you to move in this direction?* (Growth) Connection Honesty (Self-Expression) Fun Authenticity Spontaneity Risk Adventure Creativity (Independence) (Courage)

In math class the next day, just thinking about raising her hand brought a rush of blood to Bella's cheeks. She felt like she was doomed, but she rechecked her values compass and reminded herself where she wanted to go. When the teacher asked a question that nobody seemed to know the answer to, Bella inched her hand upward into the void.

It took several minutes for her heart to stop pounding and her cheeks to cool down, but Bella survived the exposure. She couldn't be sure, but it seemed as though her blushing didn't matter that much to the class. She filled out her post-exposure chart as soon as she got home from school.

Example: Bella's Post-Exposure Chart

Did I meet my realistic goal? How?	Yes! I raised my hand and answered the question.
Did I use safety behaviors? What did I do instead?	No. I faced the teacher and did not cover my face with makeup or my hands.
How did I move toward my values?	I participated in class. That will help me get a better grade and help me get into college.
What was the actual outcome?	I blushed a LOT! But hardly anyone was even looking. The people who did look didn't react badly.
What have I learned?	I can answer questions in class even though I'm blushing.

It was halfway through May, and school would be letting out in a few weeks. Bella knew that if she didn't line up a job soon, she might be unemployed all summer. She decided to move up her ladder a couple of rungs and get a job application. Doing that was rated an 8, and Bella wasn't looking forward to it one bit.

But Bella didn't want to go back to her old avoidance behavior; she'd never get a job that way. To prepare herself, Bella took the time to fill out the pre-exposure chart.

Example: Bella's Pre-Exposure Chart, Part A

Exposure	*What feared situation are you facing?* Asking for application at a coffee shop
Anxious Prediction	*What are you afraid will happen?* I'll blush and the barista will think I'm uncool.
Distortions	*What distorted thinking does your anxious prediction rely on?* ☑ Catastrophizing (assuming the worst possible outcome) ☑ Discounting the positive (refusing to take credit when you deserve it) ☑ Labeling (putting a negative name on yourself) ☐ Spotlighting (thinking everybody is watching you and/or how you feel inside shows on the outside) ☑ Mind reading (guessing what others are thinking or will think) ☐ Negative comparison (comparing yourself to others who are popular or successful) ☑ Social perfectionism (the belief that mistakes are unacceptable)
Safety Behavior	*What would you normally do to prevent your anxious prediction from happening?* I can't blush or show any signs of anxiety.

Realistic Goal	*What can you accomplish even though you feel anxious?* Getting the application
Coping Thought	*What can you remind yourself of when you are feeling the most anxious?* I can survive a few seconds of embarrassment to move me closer to my goal.
Values	*What motivates you to move in this direction?* Growth　　　　Connection　　　　Honesty　　　　Self-Expression Fun　　　　Authenticity　　　　Spontaneity　　　　Risk Adventure　　　　Creativity　　　　(Independence)　　　　(Courage)

Filling out the form really helped. It gave Bella just enough clarity and confidence to get her feet moving in the direction of the coffee shop.

Bella felt good. Getting the application without being humiliated was a surprise; none of her awful predictions had come true. "Even though I was blushing, the manager didn't notice," Bella thought. "Gotta love makeup!"

Oops!

There was something Bella had conveniently forgotten about. This time, she was wearing extra-heavy foundation to hide her blushing. If nobody could see her blushing, then she wasn't really exposed.

All shy people use sneaky or subtle avoidances that keep them from being completely exposed. Using tons of deodorant to hide sweating, mumbling to avoid being heard, not initiating conversation at a party, and drinking to lower inhibitions are all techniques for playing it safe. These safety behaviors trick us into thinking we are engaged in the world when we are actually avoiding it.

For Bella to keep climbing her ladder toward her goal of getting a job, she was going to have to repeat this exposure without using her safety behavior, without makeup. So she went to another branch of the coffee shop chain to ask for an application. This barista was a guy who looked right at her as the color rose in her face. Bella felt embarrassed, but he acted normal and told her the shop was a cool place to work. If Bella hadn't left right away, they might even have had a longer conversation. Bella felt relieved.

Here's the chart she filled out to evaluate her experience.

Example: Bella's Post-Exposure Chart

Did I meet my realistic goal? How?	Yes. I got the application.
Did I use safety behaviors? What did I do instead?	No. I did not wear heavy makeup and kept from covering up my face.
How did I move toward my values?	This is a step toward independence.
What was the actual outcome?	I did blush but he didn't seem to notice. And I got the application!
What have I learned?	Blushing does not have to stop me from doing things.

After she filled out the worksheet, Bella filled out her application. But as satisfying as it was to have her potential future job in hand, the thought of actually going in for an interview was terrifying. A solid 10! "I just can't do it," Bella thought. She was dead certain of what would happen to her in a job interview.

But Bella couldn't bear the thought of being unemployed and broke all summer. She decided that getting a shot at the long-term gain was worth some possible short-term pain. She and her friend Sandra got appointments to be interviewed at the coffee shop the same morning. Sandra dropped a bombshell at the last minute when she insisted that Bella comb her hair out of her face, saying, "So we can see you!"

"That's just my hairstyle," Bella argued. Then she quickly realized that hiding behind her hair was a safety behavior, so before they left, she added it to her chart.

Example: Bella's Pre-Exposure Chart, Part A

Exposure	What feared situation are you facing? Going for a job interview
Perfectionist Goal	How do you think you should act and appear in this situation? Relaxed and confident
Anxious Prediction	What are you afraid will happen? The manager will see me blushing and know I'm not fit to work behind the counter.
Distortions	What distorted thinking does your anxious prediction rely on? ☑ Catastrophizing (assuming the worst possible outcome) ☐ Discounting the positive (refusing to take credit when you deserve it) ☐ Labeling (putting a negative name on yourself) ☑ Spotlighting (thinking everybody is watching you and/or how you feel inside shows on the outside) ☑ Mind reading (guessing what others are thinking or will think) ☐ Negative comparison (comparing yourself to others who are popular or successful) ☑ Social perfectionism (the belief that mistakes are unacceptable)
Safety Behavior	What would you normally do to prevent your anxious prediction from happening? Wear make up and cover my face with hair.

Example: Bella's Pre-Exposure Chart, Part B

Realistic Goal	*What can you accomplish even though you feel anxious?* Going through with the interview
Coping Thought	*What can you remind yourself of when you are feeling the most anxious?* The worst thing that can happen is that I won't get the job.
Values	*What motivates you to move in this direction?* Growth Connection Honesty Self-Expression Fun Authenticity Spontaneity Risk Adventure Creativity (Independence) (Courage)

Going into the interview with her hair pulled back felt like the hardest thing Bella had ever done in her life. Here's the worksheet Bella filled out after the interview.

Example: Bella's Post-Exposure Chart

Did I meet my realistic goal? How?	Yes. I made it through the interview.
Did I use safety behaviors? What did I do instead?	No. I let my face show the whole time!
How did I move toward my values?	I took a step toward independence.
What was the actual outcome?	I definitely blushed, but I made it through the interview. The manager seemed to like me.
What have I learned?	I am pretty sure she noticed my blushing, but she didn't seem to think it was a reason not to hire me.

As it turned out, Bella didn't get that job. But she continued to go to interviews until she was hired. A funny thing Bella noticed about the ladder, though: the higher she climbed, the more rungs there seemed to be. Working a busy shift at a new job and dealing with people all day long rated 11 on her exposure ladder. Off the chart! But after what Bella had gone through, it was manageable.

Her new experience has prompted some new, confident thoughts that speak almost as loudly as the anxious ones. By following her values compass, she is learning to accept herself, as well as the nickname her new boss gave her—Blushing Bella.

Of course, your exposures won't always go smoothly. In the next chapter, we'll look at common problems that arise and what to do about them.

Chapter 13

Troubleshooting

What to Do When You Get Stuck

Exposures, like the rest of our lives, don't always go as we plan. In this chapter we will explore the three most common problems that happen during exposures and how to deal with them.

You Didn't Follow Through on the Exposure

You planned an exposure and were psyched to do it, but when you got into the situation you felt much more anxious than you had predicted. Your impulse to avoid took over and you bailed. What to do?

It is possible that you picked something too high on your ladder. If you think that is the case, pick a lower rung. If you do not have anything lower, brainstorm and see if you can come up with something.

For example, Lucia, who thinks she is a boring conversationalist, planned to join a couple of friends at lunch and share two things she did over the weekend. She did join her friends, but when the time came for her to talk, she got sweaty and started thinking it would sound weird to suddenly start talking about herself. Before the exposure, she had thought this would be pretty easy, and she did not have anything else on her ladder. To move it down a rung for next time, Lucia came up with two ideas:

1. She could change the situation by choosing people she felt more comfortable with or talking with one person instead of two.

2. She could change what she was going to do by asking two questions, which was easier for her, and sharing just one thing she did over the weekend.

Lucia went with the first option. She did the same exposure again, but this time with relatives who were coming over for dinner at her house.

Remember that it is perfectly normal to get anxious. In fact, if you are really anxious, you have picked something that you really need to work on. Conversely, if you aren't feeling anxious, you're ready for a higher rung. It is also normal that the more you do an exposure, the less anxious you will become and the more confidence you will gain, so at least you have that to look forward to.

Another solution to this problem is to get yourself a coach; sometimes involving a friend or even a parent can help you do your exposure. Just telling someone what you plan to do can help you stick to it. Depending on what your exposure is, you may be able to get someone to go with you when you do it. For example, when Bella went for a job interview, which she rated as a 10 in scariness, she asked Sandra to come along and wait outside, to give her support afterward if she needed it.

You're Still Anxious After Multiple Exposures

After repeating an exposure multiple times, you're still just as anxious as you were the first time.

Usually when you do repeated exposures you will experience a decrease, even if only a slight one, in your anxiety. When this doesn't happen, naturally it can be discouraging. But before you give up and go back to avoiding that situation again, take a look at what could be hanging you up.

Are you doing a safety behavior? You wouldn't necessarily be aware of it if you were, so take a hard look at how you have been approaching the exposures. Are you protecting yourself in some way from an embarrassing result? If you get through the situation without experiencing the actual risks, you will also miss the rewards. Remember, safety behaviors are like water wings. You are in the water, but you believe the only reason you are not drowning is that you're wearing them. Your fear of water isn't going to diminish until you actually have to paddle and kick to stay afloat.

When Bella went to the job interview wearing heavy makeup to hide her face, the makeup made it impossible for Bella to (1) test the probability that people would notice and/ or comment on her blushing and (2) practice her ability to cope if they did notice and comment. Doing exposures while maintaining your safety behaviors is like trying to learn how to ride a bike without ever taking off the training wheels.

If multiple repetitions of an exposure don't help your confidence, you may be getting highjacked by disastrous distortions, those warped ways of thinking we discussed in chapter 5. Like a funhouse mirror, they are an inaccurate way of viewing yourself and the world.

In this case, the first disastrous distortion to consider is spotlighting. You may be so self-conscious, so aware of everything that you say or do, that you have trouble getting into the swing of things. In a way, spotlighting is like another safety behavior. You are watching yourself super carefully so that you don't mess up. Try taking the spotlight off yourself. Uncensor yourself; say what comes to mind. Pay attention to the people and the environment around you.

And while you are paying attention, make sure you are not discounting the positive things that happen during your exposure. Do you hyperfocus on any facial expression that might reflect boredom, disgust, disappointment, or irritation, and miss the expressions that indicate a positive response to you? It's common for socially anxious teens to misinterpret people's innocent facial expressions as being judgmental.

If you're not practicing safety behaviors or getting caught up in disastrous distortions, then it's possible the situation you are practicing is one you will always feel anxious in. In some cases, repeated exposure won't get rid of anxiety no matter how much you practice. Some activities are scary, but we do them anyway. As an extreme example, you might ride the roller coaster over and over, year after year, and yet your heart still pounds, you still scream, and you still hang on to the grab bar for dear life. Public speakers and stage performers still get butterflies in their stomachs before they step out in front of audiences, even after years of experience. We keep right on doing things that make us scared or nervous because of the rewards—the exhilaration of the G forces on the roller coaster or an audience's applause. Anxiety is an essential, normal part of the human experience. If you've done an exposure repeated times, anxious or not, you are now doing something you have avoided in the past.

You Got Poor Results

You do your exposure and things go wrong—horribly, terribly wrong!

The most common thing that might make you think your exposure went wrong is when your anxious prediction comes true. Here are some examples:

> You blush and sweat, and someone comments on it by saying something like, "Look at you blushing; how cute!"

> Your exposure is to start a conversation with someone. After you say hi, your mind really does go blank, and you stand there not saying anything more, just smiling, while the person walks away.

> You speak up in English class, giving an opinion on the book your class is reading, and another student rudely disagrees with you.

> You comment on social media and someone comments back that you're stupid.

Are you catastrophizing? Teens with social anxiety are hypersensitive to rejection and embarrassment. When something goes wrong, they tend to feel it really was catastrophic, that they are doomed to a life of ridicule and rejection. As we know from chapter 5, catastrophic thinking is a type of disastrous distortion that leads to more anxious feelings and more avoidance. Trusting catastrophic thoughts to guide you is like letting your anxieties sit in the driver's seat.

If you suspect yourself of catastrophizing, ask yourself these challenge questions:

> *What did I do that was okay?*

> *What value am I moving toward?*

> *Am I 100 percent certain that my catastrophic thought is true?*

> *What is a more likely prediction?*

The fact is, learning to navigate bumps in the road will both help you become a better driver and get you where you want to go.

Catastrophe or not, being criticized is painful. When things go wrong, it is an excellent opportunity to practice coping with criticism. For example, if someone called your social media post "stupid," how can you stand up for yourself? Was your comment literally stupid? Or were you freely expressing yourself and they did not like what you expressed? You can stand up for yourself by saying something like, "That's my opinion; you don't have to agree." Or you can simply ignore the comment and move on. Some people use social media to pick fights and you don't need to engage with them. Standing up for yourself isn't about changing others; it's about being true to yourself no matter what others think or say.

Being judged or criticized, and learning to cope with it, is part of any exposure we choose to do because that's how we master social anxiety. When coping gets difficult, return to the exercises in chapter 9 and remind yourself that there is something worse than a "bad" outcome: no outcome, as in *not doing the exposure at all*. If you put yourself in a situation where things could go horribly wrong, and they actually do, congratulate yourself. By exposing yourself to criticism, you lived according to your values and moved toward your goal. Mission accomplished!

The Go-to Solution

Regardless of the problem you're having with your exposures—overwhelming fear, persistent anxiety, or worst-case outcomes—the single most effective troubleshooting technique is to revisit your exposure chart. "What?" you may say. "I really need to fill those out? Like a test or a school assignment?"

Skipping or skimming the worksheets is tempting. Nobody enjoys paperwork. A lot of teens feel that they can wing it, that this stuff is so simple, that writing everything down is a waste of time. But there is a clinically proven reason why you should fill out your worksheet for every exposure. Without a worksheet, under pressure, you are far more likely to go back to your old automatic thoughts and safety behaviors. And without taking the time to fill in the post-exposure chart, you are more likely to obsess about not meeting a perfectionist goal. The post-exposure chart is designed to help you see the experience in a new way—that is, moving toward your values and going after what is important to you.

As an experiment, try charting the exposure you're having trouble with, starting with part A of the pre-exposure worksheet, which is all about your fears and distortions. Take the time to think each question through, answering as honestly as you can. Part A can be pretty tough to get through, but making an honest assessment of your unproductive thoughts, goals, and behaviors is a necessary step before you can come up with new ones. Part B of the pre-exposure worksheet is your cheerleading section. When the going gets tough, what can you tell yourself that will keep you from retreating? Remember to focus on what you can actually accomplish and why you are doing this in the first place.

Did you fill it out? Great! Review the worksheet as often as necessary. Share it with a trusted friend or an understanding parent. Exposures are like tests; better preparation tends to get better results. And once you've done an exposure, remember to fill out the post-exposure chart. If you feel the exposure went badly, your answers to those questions will help you recover. If you feel the exposure went well, your answers will help set you up for the next rung on your ladder.

Managing your fears with worksheets and ladders can feel unnatural and tedious at first, especially before you begin enjoying the rewards your hard work will bring you. As you gain momentum and start getting closer to your goals, you'll begin to understand your anxiety in a new way. Rather than fighting your fear, you'll learn to lean into it. What do I mean by "lean into the fear"? Read the next chapter to find out!

Above and Beyond

How Mistakes Make You Stronger

Chapter 14

Up until now, I've been showing you how putting yourself into carefully planned situations that expose you to the possibility of being embarrassed will move you toward your goals and help you live according to your personal values. I hope by now you've climbed a ladder or two and gotten a taste of what you are capable of. In this last chapter, I'm going to suggest a way to supercharge your progress, a way to go above and beyond the ladder.

Making Mistakes on Purpose

The idea is simple. Instead of exposing yourself to the *possibility* of being embarrassed, expose yourself to the *certainty* of being embarrassed. This means making intentional mistakes and purposely allowing yourself to be judged and criticized, even rejected by others. You might ask a "stupid" question. You might purposely bore someone. You might ask someone to do something with you that you know they will say no to.

"On purpose?" you're thinking. "Are you kidding?"

It's not as crazy as it sounds. As anyone who's ever mastered a sport knows, to get better, we have to challenge ourselves *beyond* our ability. If you watch skateboarders, for example, you'll see they're always trying more difficult moves that they fail at repeatedly. That's why skaters say, "If you're not falling, you're not skating."

Just as falling is part of skating, making mistakes is part of living. Nobody gets a free pass from being judged and criticized. We reach our goals by learning how to recover from our mistakes, not by avoiding them. You can wait until you make a mistake accidentally or you can make one purposely so you can practice recovering. Guess which method gets the best results?

So what kind of mistakes am I talking about? Here are some above-and-beyond ideas:

Spray water under your arms and on your forehead to mimic excessive sweat.

Make your hands shake while you are drinking something.

Post a goofy picture of yourself on social media.

At your favorite clothing store, try on clothes inside out and ask the clerk how you look.

At a convenience store, pay with a pocketful of change.

Intentionally misspell a word in a social media post.

When the teacher asks the class a question, raise your hand and answer it wrong.

Call a pet store and ask if they sell dog food.

Walk into a movie theater and sit in front of someone after the movie has started.

Set your phone alarm to go off an hour into the movie.

Buy an ice cream cone, drop it, and ask for another one for free.

You get the idea. If the thought of a mistake makes you feel anxious, chances are it would be a great "above and beyond" exposure.

Here are examples for Lucia and Chris.

Lucia thinks she is boring. She is afraid to draw attention to herself for fear that others will judge her. What does she do?

She interrupts people on purpose.

She yells across the hall to say hi to someone.

She shares parts of her day that she knows are boring.

Chris is worried he will say something wrong and make a fool of himself. What does he do?

He calls someone by the wrong name on purpose.

He mispronounces a common word.

He orders something that he knows the restaurant doesn't serve.

Willing to Fall

The great difficulty we have with purposely messing up in others' eyes is that, from the viewpoint of the brain-within-a-brain that runs our nervous system, what I call the monkey mind, any mistake could be fatal. *Say or do the wrong thing and the whole world will turn against you.* This distortion is the most disastrous of them all, because it keeps you hiding out, playing it safe, and never learning how to recover from and cope with mistakes. Since the only way to acquire confidence in knowing you can handle others' judgments is to experience being judged. You must move out of your comfort zone, where you know you're going to make mistakes and draw criticism. The best way to get socially confident is to purposely make social mistakes.

You may thinking, "Even if that's true, is it worth it?" Was it worth it when you learned to walk? As a baby, you fell when you tried to stand up. You fell and you cried a lot. But you kept getting up because you had an inborn drive to walk on your own across the room into your parents' arms. You learned how to recover from falling, how to be resilient. And ultimately, you became confident in your ability to walk, and eventually to run.

Your drive to connect with others is just as inborn as your drive to walk was. We all need to belong. Are you willing to fall to get there?

Conclusion

Understanding your social anxiety can help you realize that there are millions of others exactly like you. Recognizing how distorted thoughts drive feelings and behaviors can help you question your thoughts and break the chain of avoidance. By facing fears one at a time, using coping strategies, and taking manageable risks, you can move from a life limited by social anxiety to one in which you can go where you want and have the friends you deserve.

If you have tried the techniques outlined in this book, hopefully you've experienced a decrease in your social anxiety and are able to do some things that you were avoiding before. To maintain the gains you have made, continue to practice your coping thoughts and pushing yourself to keep doing exposures. You are like an athlete in training; if you stop exercising, your muscles will weaken. If you challenge yourself with regular workouts, you will get stronger.

There's no guarantee that your social anxiety will completely go away. Even after significant progress, you will undoubtedly still have days when you want to avoid situations that didn't bother you at all the day before. This is normal. Your level of anxiety, like other moods, can be influenced by lack of sleep, what you eat, menstrual cycle, and the use of alcohol and drugs, to mention just a few factors. If you can identify what seems to make you feel more anxious, you can help yourself by regulating that influence. In fact, just identifying it can bring some relief. For example, if you notice that you feel more anxious after a poor night's sleep, you can remind yourself that you will feel better when you are more rested.

Disruptive life events—like starting a new job, going to a new school or away to college, or moving to a new neighborhood or city—can all trigger an increase in social anxiety. These are all opportunities to review what you have learned in this book and practice the techniques.

So how can you tell whether you are really making progress? The best way is to look honestly at which situations you are avoiding. Your motto is "Avoid avoiding!" If you are avoiding what is important to you, you have fallen into your old traps of social perfectionism or any of the other disastrous distortions. Get out your values compass, and remember what is important to you. Then turn to the skills that helped you before; they are the same skills that will help you again. Remember that you are not alone, and *you can master social anxiety!*

For Teens and Their Parents or Guardians

About Therapy and Medication

This book is a self-help book. It explains what social anxiety is and how to get through it so that it does not get in the way of doing what you want in life. But sometimes self-help is not enough. If you are having trouble following through with the exercises and exposures in this book, or if you are doing the exercises but don't seem to be moving ahead, finding a therapist to work with may be what you need.

It is sort of like learning a sport. You might read about how the game is played and what you need to practice to get good at it, and yet still need a coach. Therapists are like coaches. They can work with you to develop the skills you need and point out things that you may not be aware of, like safety behaviors. They can also give you the encouragement to follow through with exposures that are especially challenging.

This book is based on cognitive behavioral therapy (CBT) and acceptance and commitment therapy (ACT). CBT focuses on the relationship between thoughts (cognitions), feelings, and action (behavior). A CBT therapist will help you identify and challenge the thoughts that are making you more anxious and change the behaviors that are making your problem worse. ACT is a type of CBT that focuses more on changing behavior and less on changing thoughts. The objective in ACT is to identify values and commit to actions that will lead you to live a richer, more meaningful life.

CBT and ACT are very effective for all anxiety problems, including social anxiety. If you decide to see a therapist, it is very important that you find one who is trained in CBT or ACT.

What to Ask a Therapist

You will want to feel comfortable with the therapist you see. You have every right to ask questions to make sure that the therapist you choose will be a good fit for you and has the experience to treat the issue you want to work on. These questions are good ones for you and your parent or guardian to ask:

What is your training in cognitive behavioral therapy? (Therapists will ideally be able to talk about workshops they have taken, experienced clinicians they have consulted with, organizations they belong to, and certificates they hold in CBT.)

What is your training or background in treating social anxiety?

How much of your current practice involves treating social anxiety?

Do you feel you have been effective in treating social anxiety?

What techniques do you use for social anxiety? (You want your therapist to talk about using exposure techniques and working with distorted thinking.)

If needed, are you willing to leave your office to do behavioral therapy? (Some of your exposures may require you and your therapist to be in public spaces.)

About Medication

You may be wondering or have heard about medication for social anxiety. In fact, there are medications that can help with social anxiety, as well as other types of anxiety. There are basically two types: antidepressants and benzodiazepines.

Antidepressants

You may be wondering why antidepressants are prescribed for anxiety. The reason is that the way the drug works in your brain to decrease depression decreases anxiety as well. Also, it is not uncommon for people who have social anxiety to have depression too. These medications can help with both problems.

The most common type of antidepressants are called selective serotonin reuptake inhibitors, or SSRIs. Serotonin is a brain chemical that influences mood, and these drugs work by increasing serotonin levels; they also work on other chemicals in the brain that affect mood. Some common SSRIs include fluoxetine (Prozac), paroxetine (Paxil), citalopram (Celexa), sertraline (Zoloft), escitalopram (Lexapro), and fluvoxamine (Luvox). Other antidepressants that are sometimes used are venlafaxine (Effexor), duloxetine (Cymbalta), and mirtazapine (Remeron). Each name in parenthesis is the brand name of the drug; the first name is the generic name and is based on the drug's chemical structure.

Another type of antidepressants are called tricyclic antidepressants (TCAs). These include amitriptyline (Elavil) and imipramine (Tofranil). TCAs are not prescribed as frequently as SSRIs because they have more side effects.

There are pros and cons to taking SSRIs and TCIs.

Pros

- They are not that expensive.

- Most people find it easy to take pills.

- These medications are not addictive.

- Because you take these medications every day, as opposed to only when you feel anxious, they are less likely to be used as safety behaviors.

Cons

- There can be side effects. The most common are nausea, diarrhea, constipation, drowsiness or jitteriness, dry mouth, headaches, yawning, shakiness, and sexual side effects, such as difficulty having an orgasm and/ or decreased sexual drive. Many of these side effects decrease over time. There is a black box warning for people age twenty-six and younger that SSRIs can cause increased thoughts of suicide. This is associated with people who have both anxiety and depression, not anxiety alone. There is not an increase in actual suicide attempts.

- These medications can take from four to six weeks to have a noticeable effect. Not every antidepressant works for every individual, so it might take trying more than one before finding what works.

- Going off the medication can cause uncomfortable symptoms, like dizziness, nausea, headaches, difficulty sleeping, or flu-like symptoms. If you decrease your dose slowly when going off these medications, these effects will be less intense.

- When you stop taking these medications, social anxiety symptoms often come back.

Benzodiazepines

Benzodiazepines are relaxants that work very quickly in the body and brain. People usually take them when they become anxious or panicky or when they are going into situations that make them anxious. Common benzodiazepines include alprazolam (Xanax), diazepam (Valium), lorazepam (Ativan), and clonazepam (Klonopin).

There are pros and cons to taking benzodiazepines.

Pros

- They are quick acting.

- They can be taken as needed.

- They are not that expensive.

- Most people find it easy to take pills.

Cons

- There can be side effects, like drowsiness, light-headedness, confusion, and depression.

- They can be deadly if you mix them with alcohol.

- They can become a safety behavior that you are dependent on. Even if you are not physically addicted, they can get in the way of you facing your fears and gaining confidence in yourself.

- They can become physically addicting. If there is a history of addiction in your family, you are at even higher risk of addiction to benzodiazepines.

- You can develop a tolerance when you use this medication repeatedly and the body adapts to the continued presence of this drug. This can lead to addiction because you use more and more over time with the same effect.

- If you have developed a tolerance you can have physical withdrawal, typically shakiness, sweating, diarrhea, and heart palpitations, as well as a rebound effect of heightened anxiety.

Other Medications

There may be other medications that you can take as needed that are not addictive and don't have the risk of building tolerance. Examples of these are hydroxyzine (Atarax), buspirone (Buspar), and gabapentin. You can talk to your doctor about these options.

Whether to Take Medication

Should you or shouldn't you take medication for your anxiety? Well, first of all, thinking you should or should not do anything is the wrong approach. These words imply that there is an absolute right and wrong for everyone, which is perfectionist thinking.

If you are experiencing extreme anxiety that is getting in the way of your functioning, like getting out of the house and going to school, or doing the exercises in this book, you may want to talk to your doctor about medication. It is usually a medical doctor who prescribes medication for anxiety, most commonly a family doctor, general practitioner, or psychiatrist (a medical doctor who specializes in mental health).

For those who try medication, the best results have been obtained by people who combine it with CBT. This makes sense. The medication can help lower the volume on your anxiety. The therapy will teach you skills to overcome the anxiety now and in the long run. That way, when you stop taking medication, you will be much less likely to experience a return of your social anxiety.

Helpful Resources

Books

A Teen's Guide to Getting Stuff Done: Discover Your Procrastination Type, Stop Putting Things Off, and Reach Your Goals by Jennifer Shannon

The Anxiety Survival Guide for Teens: CBT Skills to Overcome Fear, Worry, and Panic by Jennifer Shannon

Freeing Your Child from Anxiety: Powerful, Practical Solutions to Overcome Your Child's Fears, Worries, and Phobias by Tamar Chansky

If Your Adolescent Has an Anxiety Disorder: An Essential Resource for Parents by Edna Foa and Linda Wasmer Andrews

My Anxious Mind: A Teen's Guide to Managing Anxiety and Panic by Michael Tompkins and Katherine Martinez

Websites

These sites offer information about anxiety, CBT, and ACT.

Academy of Cognitive Therapy (ACT): www.academyofct.org

This organization helps people access cognitive therapy resources, learn more about mental health disorders, and find a certified cognitive therapist.

Anxiety Disorders Association of America: adaa.org

This organization is dedicated to spreading awareness about the severity of anxiety disorders and effective treatments.

Association for Behavioral and Cognitive Therapies: abct.org

This organization focuses on promoting ongoing research regarding the effectiveness of therapies used to treat a variety of mental health conditions.

Overcoming Teen Anxiety: www.overcomingteenanxiety.com

This is Jennifer Shannon's website that has resources for teens and printable worksheets to help with anxiety and procrastination.

Paruresis

If you have ever had trouble peeing in a public restroom, you are not alone. Most of us have experienced this at some time in our lives. The technical term for this problem is *paruresis* (pronounced par-yu-REE-sis). It is commonly referred to as "shy bladder" or "bashful bladder," and it can range from mild to quite severe.

Millions of people suffer from paruresis, but they usually suffer alone because they are embarrassed to tell anyone. Shy bladder is caused by social anxiety. Sufferers are usually afraid of being watched, listened to, and in some way negatively judged. Their anxiety makes it impossible to allow urine to flow, no matter how full the bladder is. So not only is this problem embarrassing, but it can also be very painful and potentially dangerous, leading to urinary tract infections and swelling of your kidneys.

As we know, socially anxious teens will always attempt to avoid situations that make them anxious: in this case, peeing in a public facility, or even at home when there are other people around. This avoidance can really get in the way of living their lives and doing the things that are important to them. Going to restaurants, to friends' houses, to parties, or anywhere can be a big problem.

This self-test can help you figure out how much of a problem paruresis is for you.

	Yes	No
Do you have a marked and persistent fear of using public restrooms while others are present?		
Do you experience problems starting your urine in public facilities when others are present?		
Do you worry about what other people are thinking when you are trying to urinate?		
Are you able to urinate at home even though you can't do so away from home?		
Are you concerned about being humiliated or embarrassed by problems passing urine?		
Does attempting to urinate in public restrooms always, or almost always, make you anxious?		
Does the fear of using public restrooms seem silly or unreasonable to you?		
Do you avoid urinating in public restrooms and/or do you endure using public restrooms with intense anxiety and distress?		
Does your avoidance of public restrooms, or anxiety and distress about using them, interfere significantly with your relationships, social activities, or work?		
Has a doctor ruled out a physical cause for your difficulties urinating in public?		

The more yes answers you gave, the more of a problem paruresis probably is for you. The good news is that the problem is very treatable with many of the same strategies outlined in this book. Because of the unique brain-bladder connection, however, there are specific ways to go about treating paruresis that are not covered here. These resources can help you learn more:

International Paruresis Association: paruresis.org

Shy Bladder Center: shybladder.org

Shy Bladder Syndrome: Your Step-by-Step Guide to Overcoming Paruresis by Steven Soifer, George Zgourides, Joseph Himle, and Nancy L. Pickering

Other Common Types of Anxiety

People with social anxiety often have other types of anxiety as well. Here is a list of the most common types and some typical symptoms. Got to http://www.newharbinger.com/48015 to download a brief quiz that will help you identify which types of anxiety you may suffer from. While many of the exercises in this book can help with the problems listed below, it is best to learn about specific tools and exercises for each type of anxiety. The websites on page 156 may also be helpful for these types of anxiety.

Panic Attacks

> Suddenly feeling really scared when you don't expect it

> Physical sensations like racing heart, trouble catching your breath, or dizziness

> Fear of going crazy, dying, or losing control

> Fear of leaving your home

> Feeling trapped when in a store or in class

General Anxiety

> Worries that are hard to control

> Worry that you or someone you love might get hurt or die

> Worry about natural disasters like earthquakes, tsunamis, or hurricanes

> Worry about homework assignments, tests, or getting in trouble at school

> Worry about being late to things

> Physical symptoms like stomachaches and headaches

Phobias

> Fear of specific places like elevators, heights, or bodies of water

> Fear of certain animals or insects

> Fear of needles or blood

> Fear of vomiting

Obsessive-Compulsive Disorder

Unwanted and unpleasant thoughts that get stuck in your head

Fear of germs or getting dirty

Worry that you hurt someone or did something bad

Need for things to be even or just so

Need to repeat certain actions even when you know it does not make sense

Separation Anxiety

Fear of being along or sleeping alone

Fear of being away from your parents

Anxiety when you go to school, on field trips, or away overnight

Post-Traumatic Stress Disorder

Intense fear, helplessness, and avoidance in response to a traumatic event

Reexperiencing the trauma through flashbacks or nightmares

Feeling numb and avoiding people, places, or activities that are reminders of the trauma

Jennifer Shannon, LMFT, is a psychotherapist, and author of *Don't Feed the Monkey Mind*, *The Anxiety Survival Guide for Teens*, and *A Teen's Guide to Getting Stuff Done*. She is a diplomate of the Academy of Cognitive Therapy.

Illustrator **Doug Shannon** is a freelance cartoonist.

More  Instant Help Books for Teens

An Imprint of New Harbinger Publications

Did you know there are **free tools** you can download for this book?

Free tools are things like **worksheets**, **guided meditation exercises**, and **more** that will help you get the most out of your book.

You can download free tools for this book— whether you bought or borrowed it, in any format, from any source—from the New Harbinger website. All you need is a NewHarbinger.com account. Just use the URL provided in this book to view the free tools that are available for it. Then, click on the "download" button for the free tool you want, and follow the prompts that appear to log in to your NewHarbinger.com account and download the material.

You can also save the free tools for this book to your **Free Tools Library** so you can access them again anytime, just by logging in to your account! Just look for this button on the book's free tools page.

+ Save this to my free tools library

If you need help accessing or downloading free tools, visit **newharbinger.com/faq** or contact us at **customerservice@newharbinger.com**.